4.73

W9-ARA-768

Bibliographical Guide to the Study of the
Literature of the U. S. A.

BIBLIOGRAPHICAL GUIDE TO THE STUDY OF THE LITERATURE OF THE U. S. A.

SECOND EDITION
Revised and Enlarged

CLARENCE GOHDES

DUKE UNIVERSITY PRESS *Durham, N. C.*

© 1959, 1963, Duke University Press

Library of Congress Catalog Card number 63-18575

Cambridge University Press, London, N. W. 1, England

Printed in the United States of America
by The Seeman Printery, Inc., Durham, N. C.

23393

To
JAY BROADUS HUBBELL

PREFACE

The present volume undertakes to provide lists of books which will aid the professional student of the literature of the United States in the acquiring of information and in the techniques of research. It is believed that it will prove useful to college teachers of American literature, to reference librarians, and, more especially, to graduate students writing master's or doctor's theses. In its way, it is comparable to the bibliographical guides to English literature compiled by Arthur G. Kennedy, Tom P. Cross, and John W. Spargo. Their manuals, with varying emphasis and method, contain material on American as well as British literature, but their treatment of the former is relatively incidental and for sound reasons has proved unsatisfactory to Americanists. This book is the first of its kind to see print.

In addition to materials having to do with methods of research and with American literature in its several phases, essential tools are herein listed for the study of American history, biography, art, religion, philosophy, etc., not only because of the patent need for backgrounds but also because of the special interests of a large number of students or scholars who investigate the literature of the United States in interdepartmental programs usually spoken of as *American Studies* or *American Civilization*. Historians of ideas will find that their favored approach has also been recognized in the selection of titles for this guide. Calculated consideration has, furthermore, been given to American literature as a part of comparative studies, and a special section is devoted to the relationship of the national letters with foreign countries and foreign literatures. The compiler has borne in mind not only the manifest importance of foreign influences upon the *belles-lettres* of the United States but the repercussions, so to speak, of the national literature in foreign countries. It is hoped that this guide will prove helpful to such professional students of its subject as are now at work in Japan, Germany, and the other countries where American Studies constitute a part of academic curricula.

The various headings for the individual sections of the guide will usually provide sufficient direction to the reader, but indexes of subjects and of authors, compilers, or editors are appended as additional aids to the locating of information. In many cases the individual items that make up the contents of this book are recorded in "short title" style, but whenever a subtitle seemed advantageous in calling attention to the contents or purpose of a given work it has been printed.

By abandoning an alphabetical order for the works listed in this guide I have at times been able to begin the various sections with the most generally used bibliographies or to group titles which have a special affiliation. For example, in Section 32, "American Literature in Relations with Other Countries and Literatures," all the works dealing with the relationship with France appear in consecutive order rather than scattered as they would be if an alphabetical arrangement were followed. Cross-references are supplied at the ends of various sections calling attention to important items classified elsewhere, but the index of subjects will usually provide further aid in locating items dealing in part with a given topic. Very few anthologies have been included, and such as do appear are listed because of their special editorial or bibliographical contents.

The long dashes indicate that publication is still in process as of March, 1963. The dates following semicolons indicate the year of a reprinting. The reader should be warned, however, that the indication of reprints is bound to prove incomplete, for so many books of a scholarly or semi-scholarly sort are now being reproduced by offset that the record can never be kept up to date.

In preparing this revised and expanded edition I have been astounded at the vast number of reprints waiting to be recorded and bewildered by the array of new titles demanding inclusion. Every page of the original edition has been changed except two. Entirely new is the Appendix, which is intended to help the reader to find the books which will best start him off in the pursuit of biographical information concerning one hundred different authors. Many of the works listed, one hopes, will eventually be replaced by worthier studies; and more authors of note, one also hopes, will in time be added to my list. In selecting titles I, of course, have assumed the responsibility of making the final decisions, but I have had the advice of a very considerable number of the ablest scholars.

For information and suggestions of one sort or the other I am grateful to many people who have aided in compiling the present edition. Of my own colleagues at Duke Universi(/ I wish to thank especially John Alden, Robert Durden, Irving B. Holley, Jr., Richard Watson, and Robert Woody, of the History Department; Stuart Henry and H. Shelton Smith, of the Divinity School; Louise Hall and Ransom Patrick, of the Art Department; Joseph Riddel and George Williams, of the English Department; and Ashbel Brice, John Menapace, and the late William Owens, of the Duke University Press.

I am grateful also to the following scholars and experts from other institutions: Alfred O. Aldridge (Maryland), George Arms (New Mexico), Roger Asselineau (Paris), Roy P. Basler (Library of Congress), Charles Boewe (Pennsylvania), Robert A. Bone (U.C.L.A.), Fredson Bowers (Virginia), Clarence A. Brown (Marquette), Milton Byrd (Northern Michigan), Harry H. Clark (Wisconsin), Oral S. Coad (Douglass), Hennig Cohen (Pennsylvania), F. W. Conner (Alabama), Alexander Cowie (Wesleyan), E. V. K. Dobbie (Columbia), Richard Dorson (Indiana), Bernard Duffey (Michigan State), David Erdman (N. Y. Public Library), Marvin Felheim (Michigan), Max Fisch (Illinois), Horst Frenz (Indiana), Werner P. Friederich (North Carolina), Hans Galinsky (Mainz), Frederick L. Gwynn (Trinity), James D. Hart (California, Berkeley), Ima H. Herron (Southern Methodist), C. Hugh Holman (North Carolina), Theodore Hornberger (Pennsylvania), Helen D. Jones (Library of Congress), Joseph Jones (Texas), Albert R. Kitzhaber (Oregon), Robert H. Land (Library of Congress), Lewis Leary (Columbia), Raven I. McDavid, Jr. (Chicago), James B. Meriwether (North Carolina), Perry Miller (Harvard), Alton C. Morris (Florida), Frank L. Mott (Missouri),

Henry Pochmann (Wisconsin), Lawrence C. Powell (U.C.L.A.), S. J. Riccardi (N. Y. Public Library), Edgar P. Richardson (Winterthur Museum), Lyon C. Richardson (Western Reserve), Walter Rideout (Northwestern), Albert J. Robbins (Indiana), Louis Rubin (Hollins), Ernest Samuels (Northwestern), Rollo Silver (Simmons), Louis P. Simpson (Louisiana), Sigmund Skard (Oslo), Nelle Smither (Douglass), Theodore Spencer (Ohio Wesleyan), David H. Stam (N. Y. Public Library), Madeleine B. Stern (N. Y. City), Floyd Stovall (Virginia), Heinrich Straumann (Zurich), Frederick B. Tolles (Swarthmore), Robert Walker (George Washington), Edward N. Waters (Library of Congress), and Harvey Wish (Western Reserve).

No words can ever express how grateful I am for the help received from members of the staff of the Duke University Library. Their patience was given the acid test by my multitude of inquiries. Especially kind to me have been Gertrude Merritt, Edwin J. Hix, and the wizards of the Reference Department: Florence E. Blakely, Mary W. Canada, Ardie Lee Kelly, and Mary Frances Morris. And, finally, I bow in admiration as well as gratitude to Constance Winchell (Columbia University Library), whose compilations so often have served as my bibliographical Bible.

Duke University   CLARENCE GOHDES
March, 1963

TABLE OF CONTENTS

Bibliographical Guide to the Study of the
Literature of the U. S. A.

1. AIDS TO INFORMATION ON ALL SUBJECTS

1.1   Besterman, Theodore.   A world bibliography of bibliographies: and of bibliographical catalogues, calendars, abstracts, digests, indexes, and the like.   3d ed.   4 v.   Geneva, [1955-1956]; N.Y., 1960.
International in scope, this work lists by subjects separately published bibliographies in all fields—from "academic writings" to "zoology."   V. 4 is an index.   This is the most comprehensive bibliographical guide available.

1.2   Bibliographic index: a cumulative bibliography of bibliographies 1937——.   N.Y., 1945——.
Issued quarterly; cumulated annually.   Separate bibliographies and bibliographies in books as well as in about 1500 periodicals are listed under several thousand different headings.

1.3   Winchell, Constance.   Guide to reference books.   7th ed.   Chicago, 1951.   Supplements, Chicago, 1954, 1956, 1960.
Standard guide to reference works on all subjects; periodically revised and brought up to date.

1.4   Malclès, Louise N.   Les sources du travail bibliographique.   4 v. Geneva and Lille, 1950-1958.
A well-indexed general bibliographical guide.   V. 2 and 3 are principally concerned with the humanities, and v. 4 with the exact sciences and technology.

1.5   Totok, Wilhelm, and Weitzel, Rolf.   Handbuch der bibliographischen Nachschlagewerke.   2d ed. rev.   Frankfurt a.M., [1959].
Not so full as Malclès but more systematically arranged.

1.6   Murphey, Robert W.   How and where to look it up: a guide to standard sources of information.   N.Y., [1958].
Contains numerous subject headings for more than ten thousand annotated reference sources.   Explanations of the ways to use them are prepared for the layman's needs.   Often uneven and inaccurate in details.

1.7   Walford, A. J., and Payne, L. M.   Guide to reference material.   London, 1959.
"The aim is to provide a guide to reference books and bibliographies, with emphasis on current material and material published in Britain."   The annotations are especially helpful.

1.8   American Library Association index . . . to general literature.   2d ed.
Boston and N.Y., 1901.   Supplement, Chicago, 1914.

Subject classification of books in English devoted to essays and other factual works, including biography, literary and art criticism, history, and other
social studies.   The first volume covers books published before 1900; the
supplement, books published 1900-1910.   Predecessor to the following item.

1.9   Essay and general literature index, 1900——.   N.Y., 1934——.

Now kept up to date by regularly appearing supplements; all materials indexed have appeared in book form.

1.10   Library of Congress catalog: a cumulative list of works represented
by Library of Congress cards: books: subjects 1950-1954.   20 v. Ann
Arbor, Mich., 1955.

Since 1955 continued with the Library of Congress as publisher.   Books
from the U.S. or abroad received by the Library of Congress or co-operating
libraries are classified alphabetically under headings such as "American Wit
and Humor," "English Drama," "French Literature," "Zoological Parks."
(Very useful also is *The British National Bibliography 1950——: A Subject
List of the New British Books Published in 1950——*, ed. A. J. Wells, London,
[1951]——.)

1.11   The cumulative book index: a world list of books in the English
language.   N.Y., 1933——.

An author-title-subject catalog in one alphabet of books in English published in all parts of the world since January 1, 1929.

1.12   Subject guide to books in print: an index to the Publishers' Trade
List Annual 1957——.   N.Y., [1957]——.

Under more than 20,000 topics or headings, the works currently listed in
the catalogs of all the principal U.S. publishers are recorded; volumes of poetry
and plays by a single author are omitted.

1.13   The national union catalog of manuscript collections 1959-1961.   Ann
Arbor, Mich., [1962].

Reproduces cards for about 7,300 manuscript collections issued by the
Library of Congress during the three years.   The names and subjects covered
by the collections are indexed.   First volume of a contemplated series to be
compiled by the L. of C. but based on reports from about 400 repositories.

1.14   Hamer, Philip M., ed. A guide to archives and manuscripts in the U. S.
Compiled for the National Historical Publications Commission.   New
Haven, Conn., 1961.

Indicates the chief holdings of more than 1,300 repositories arranged by
state, and is not confined to material dealing with the U. S.

1.15   American library directory.   23d ed.   N.Y., 1962.

A classified list of 14,514 libraries with names of librarians, and statistical
data; compiled biennially.

1.16   Ash, Lee. Subject collections: a guide to special book collections and subject emphases as reported by university, college, public and special libraries in the U.S., the Territories, and Canada. 2d ed. rev. N.Y., 1961.

The intention is to revise this work triennially.

1.17   Brummel, L., and Egger, E. Guide to union catalogues and international loan centers. Amsterdam, 1962.

1.18   Bulletin of bibliography. April, 1897——.

A periodical which specializes in publishing check lists and records of magazines newly started or ended. From October, 1909, to May-August, 1953, it carried a quarterly Dramatic Index of periodical articles (chiefly from popular magazines) concerned with all aspects of the theater.

1.19   Union list of microfilms: cumulation 1949-1959. 2 v. Ann Arbor, Mich., 1961.

Supplements keep this record closer to date. Co-operating libraries report their microfilm accessions for this work. Theses from American universities are no longer included. (See 1.23, *Dissertation Abstracts,* formerly *Microfilm Abstracts.*)

1.20   Tilton, Eva M. A union list of publications in opaque microforms. N.Y., 1959. Supplement, 1961.

Records American publishers' listings of microcard, etc., reproductions through December, 1958. The supplement carries on and includes listings of European publishers also.

1.21   Guide to microforms in print 1961——. Washington, 1961——.

"Lists or refers to all that is available in microform from domestic (U.S.A.) commercial publishers. Titles or projects of some non-commercial publishers are also included." Beginning in 1962, an annual *Subject Guide to Microforms in Print* has appeared as a companion to the above.

1.22   Doctoral dissertations accepted by American universities 1933-34— 1954-55. 17 v. N.Y., 1934-1955.

Covers doctoral theses in all fields. The preliminary matter in each volume contains a list of current university serials which publish abstracts of theses. Superseded by "Index to American Doctoral Dissertations," in the following item, v. 16, no. 13——. (For a special list in American literature, see 20.9, Woodress.)

1.23   Dissertation abstracts: a guide to dissertations and monographs available on microfilm. (Originally entitled Microfilm abstracts.) Ann Arbor, Mich., 1938——.

The number of co-operating universities has greatly increased, and this compilation of abstracts of dissertations which have been microfilmed now appears monthly. The Index is the standard current list of dissertations in all fields accepted by American universities.

1.24   Keller, Helen R.   The dictionary of dates.   2 v. N.Y., 1934.

1.25   Zaunmüller, Wolfram.   Bibliographisches Handbuch der Sprachwörter-
bücher.   Stuttgart, 1958.

More than 5,600 dictionaries covering about 600 languages are listed.

1.26   Vertical file index.   N.Y., 1931———.

A selective list of pamphlet material of interest to general libraries, issued
monthly, accumulated annually.   There are both a subject index and a title
index.

2. PHILOSOPHY AND GENERAL METHODOLOGY OF LITERARY AND HISTORICAL STUDY

2.1   Wellek, René, and Warren, Austin. Theory of literature. N.Y., [1949]; 1956.

Describes and criticizes the various methods of, and approaches to, the study of literature, with generalizations on literary theory, evaluation, research, and history. An excellent international bibliography is appended, with the following subtopics: "Literature and Literary Study," "The Nature of Literature," "The Function of Literature," "Literary Theory, History, and Criticism," "National, Comparative and General Literature," "The Ordering and Establishing of Evidence," "Literature and Biography," "Literature and Psychology," "Literature and Society," "Literature and Ideas," "Literature and the Other Arts," "The Analysis of the Literary Work of Art," "Euphony, Rhythm, and Meter," "Style and Stylistics," "Image, Metaphor, Symbol, and Myth," "The Nature and Modes of Fiction," "Literary Genres," "Evaluation," "Literary History," and "The Study of Literature in the Graduate School." The 1956 reprint drops the final chapter and occasionally brings the bibliography nearer to date.

2.2   Howe, George F., et al., eds. The American Historical Association's guide to historical literature. N.Y., 1961.

A somewhat uneven bibliography of selected historical works treating various nations, peoples, and religions which lists in Part I, Section A, books dealing with the methodology of history and related studies.

2.3   Greenlaw, Edwin. The province of literary history. Baltimore, [1931].

Literary history is viewed as a province distinct from that of criticism or literary biography, and certain of its problems and methods are set forth.

2.4   Boas, George. "Some problems of intellectual history." Studies in intellectual history, pp. 3-21. [Baltimore], 1953.

Points out "some of the peculiarities of historiography" and some of its problems as they pertain to the history of ideas.

2.5   Langlois, Charles V., and Seignobos, Charles. Introduction to the study of history. Tr. by G. G. Berry. N.Y., [1926].

2.6   The social sciences in historical study: a report of the committee on historiography. Social Science Research Council bulletin, no. 64. N.Y., 1954.

Discusses, among other matters, the methods dominant in various social sciences that have relevance for historians.

2.7   Collingwood, R. G. The idea of history. Oxford, 1946; N.Y., 1956.
A philosophical attempt to define the special character of historical knowledge.

2.8   Marrou, H.-I. De la connaissance historique. 2d ed. Paris, 1956.
An introduction to historical method presently in favor in certain quarters.

2.9   Jones, Howard M. The theory of American literature. Ithaca, N.Y., 1948.
Attitudes pervading scholarship on American literature from Colonial times to the present are briefly surveyed.

2.10   Hockett, Homer C. The critical method in historical research and writing. N.Y., [1955].
Both a bibliography of essential tools and a lucid guide to research in American history. Part II, "The Master's Essay," describes the processes of finding and developing a topic, note taking, outlining, making a bibliography, etc. Included also are brief surveys of American historiography, of the historical projects of the WPA and of the armed services, and of the various types of U.S. government publications. Much of the discussion of method is as pertinent for the student of literature as for the student of history. The list of chief bibliographies dealing with the history of the various regions and the several states (pp. 281-295) is especially helpful. (For methodology in the study of American history, see also the first chapters of 9.1, *Harvard Guide*.)

2.11   McDermott, John F., ed. Research opportunities in American cultural history. Lexington, Ky., [1961].
Papers by various authorities on such topics as "Travel Literature" (Thomas D. Clark), "Folklore and Cultural History" (Richard Dorson), "Middlewestern Regional Literature" (John T. Flanagan), and "The Book Trade and Publishing History" (David Kaser).

2.12   Sanders, Chauncey. An introduction to research in English literary history. N.Y., [1952].
Many of the illustrations of problems in editing, source study, etc. are taken from the American field. Part 4, "Suggestions on Thesis-writing," is elementary but clear-cut.

2.13   Morize, André. Problems and methods of literary history, with special reference to modern French literature: a guide for graduate students. Boston and N.Y., [1922].
Valuable for students of literature in any language, since it surveys the techniques employed in scholarly research.

2.14   Vigneron, Robert. Explication de textes, and its adaptation to the teaching of modern languages. Chicago, [1928].
Reprinted from *Modern Language Journal* for October, 1927. Outlines the system of *explication* as developed in France.

2.15 Hays, Edna. The college teaching of English: a bibliography 1941-1944. Pamphlet publication no. 8 of the National Council of Teachers of English. Chicago, [1946].

Continued annually in the May numbers of *College English,* 1947-1950; renewed in the October, 1957, issue with list covering 1954-1956.

2.16 Richards, Ivor A. Practical criticism: a study of literary judgment. London and N.Y., 1929; 1956.

This work is the grandfather, if not the father, of a considerable element in the recent analytical study of poetry.

2.17 Stallknecht, Newton P., and Frenz, Horst, eds. Comparative literature: method and perspective. Carbondale, Ill., 1961.

Thirteen essays on topics like definition, translation, indebtedness, relations of literature and psychology, literature and the arts, modes of criticism, and Romanticism.

2.18 Bowers, Fredson. "Textual criticism and the literary critic." Textual & literary criticism. Cambridge, 1959.

Points out the usefulness of textual criticism to aesthetic literary discussion.

3. TECHNICAL PROCEDURES IN LITERARY AND HISTORICAL RESEARCH

3.1   Studies in bibliography: papers of the Bibliographical Society of the University of Virginia, 1947——. Charlottesville, Va., 1948——.
An annual devoted to bibliographical studies pertaining especially to English and American literature. Regularly includes a selective check list of bibliographical scholarship published during the preceding year, with emphasis on printing, publishing, and textual studies. The check lists for 1949-1955 have been assembled in a decennial extra volume, v. 10, 1957.

3.2   Bowers, Fredson. Principles of bibliographical description. Princeton, N.J., 1949; N.Y., 1962.
A standard work on the methods of analyzing a book with a view to making a scientific description of it as a physical entity. Offers expert technical explanations of such matters as edition, impression, issue, state, format. Of special interest is the section on books of the 19th and 20th centuries.

3.3   Esdaile, Arundell. A student's manual of bibliography. Rev. by Roy Stokes. 3d rev. ed. London, [1954].
History of printing, methods of collating and describing books, types and arrangement of bibliographies. Often outmoded by Bowers. (For a model arrangement of an extensive single-author bibliography, see Thomas F. Currier, *A Bibliography of J. G. Whittier,* Cambridge, Mass., 1937.)

3.4   Parker, Donald. Local history: how to gather it, write it, and publish it. Rev. and ed. by Bertha E. Josephson. N.Y., 1944.
Useful for the study of minor authors of regional interest. Cf. also Philip D. Jordan, *The Nature and Practice of State and Local History,* Washington, [1958], a pamphlet issued by the Service Center for Teachers conducted by the American Historical Association.

3.5   Osborn, James M. "The search for English literary documents." English institute annual for 1939. N.Y., 1940.
Many bits of advice herein contained are applicable also to the student of Americana.

3.6   Haselden, Reginald B. Scientific aids for the study of manuscripts. [Oxford], 1935.
Contains much material on general procedures involved in studying MSS. (Practical advice on handling MSS appears also in 9.1, *Harvard Guide,* pp. 88-99.)

3.7   Greg, Walter W. The calculus of variants: an essay on textual criticism. Oxford, 1927.

A scientific treatise on the establishment of relationships among manuscripts of a given work and on the problems of handling variants.

3.8   Halsband, Robert. "Editing the letters of letter-writers." Studies in bibliography, v. 11, pp. 25-37 (1958).

Practical suggestions for handling problems presented by the editing of collections of letters. (For a splendid example of techniques applied, see *The Letters of R. W. Emerson,* ed. Ralph L. Rusk, 6 v., N.Y., 1939.)

3.9   Lewis, Chester M., and Offenhauser, William H., Jr. Microrecording. N.Y., [1956].

Description of various kinds of microrecording and copying devices and methods, including xerography. See also *Library Trends,* January, 1960.

3.10   American Library Association. Directory of library photoduplication services in the U.S., Canada, and Mexico. 2d ed., Chicago, 1962.

3.11   Ballou, Hubbard, ed. Guide to microreproduction equipment. 2d ed. Annapolis, Md., 1962.

Describes, with many illustrations, cameras, hand viewers, processors, contact printers, enlargers, etc. Issued under the auspices of the National Microfilm Association, which publishes also an annual volume of proceedings and a bimonthly *National Micro News.*

3.12   Garraty, John A. The nature of biography. N.Y., 1957.

Discusses the historical development of biography as a genre and contains a section on the methods of preparing a biography. A helpful list of sources is also provided.

3.13   Clifford, James L., ed. Biography as an art: selected criticism 1560-1960. New York, 1962.

The list of works dealing with the problems and materials of biographies adds to the usefulness of this anthology.

3.14   Brower, Reuben, ed. On translating. Cambridge, Mass., 1959.

Contains a critical bibliography. Cf. also 2.17.

3.15   Halkett, Samuel, and Laing, John. Dictionary of anonymous and pseudonymous English literature. New ed. Ed. James Kennedy *et al.* 8 v. Edinburgh and London, 1926-[1956].

Many American works are included, especially in v. 8, which covers 1900-1949. This work is a standard one for English literature, from earliest times.

3.16   Cushing, William. Anonyms: a dictionary of revealed authorship. Cambridge, Mass., 1889.

A standard work for English and American anonymous titles of the 18th and 19th centuries. (For a list of handbooks dealing with anonymously or pseudonymously published works, in various languages, see Adah V. Morris, "Anonyms and Pseudonyms, an Annotated List," *Library Quarterly,* v. 3, pp. 354-372, October, 1933.)

4. DEFINITIONS OF LITERARY AND RELATED TERMS

4.1   Wolf, Martin L.   Dictionary of the arts.   N.Y., [1951].
Briefly defines many terms used in literature, ballet, architecture, music, painting, etc.

4.2   Shipley, Joseph T., ed.   Dictionary of world literature: criticism, forms, technique.   Rev. ed.   N.Y., [1953]; Paterson, N.J., [1960].
Definitions of critical terms, with brief outlines of literary criticism in various individual countries.

4.3   Norton, Dan S., and Peters, Rushton.   A glossary of literary terms. Rev. by Meyer H. Abrams.   N.Y., [1957].
The definitions are often elementary, but clear.

4.4   Thrall, William F., and Hibbard, Addison.   A handbook to literature. Rev. by C. Hugh Holman.   N.Y., [1960].
Chiefly words and phrases "as found in criticism, rhetoric, literary history, and versification, including terminology reflecting efforts to classify literature by types, forms, and traditions."

4.5   Thompson, Elizabeth H.   American Library Association glossary of library terms: with a selection of terms in related fields.   Chicago, 1943.

4.6   Barnhart, Clarence L., ed.   The new Century handbook of English literature.   N.Y., [1956].
Contains entries on authors, titles, and characters from works of literature, etc.; includes a fair number of clear definitions.

4.7   Harvey, Paul.   The Oxford companion to English literature.   3d ed. Oxford, 1946.
A standard handbook for the study of English literature.

4.8   Glaister, Geoffrey A.   An encyclopedia of the book. Cleveland and N.Y., [1960].
Chiefly an alphabetical glossary of terms, explanations of practices, materials, etc. relating to paper-making, printing, bookbinding, and publishing. Leans heavily on the Swedish *Grafisk Uppslagbok* (1951).

4.9 Bookman's glossary. 4th ed. rev. N.Y., [1961].

Guide to terminology "used in the production and distribution of books new and old." A brief list of works on subjects reflected in the glossary appears as an appendix.

4.10 Carter, John. ABC for book-collectors. 3d ed. rev. London, [1961].

Definitions, with occasional comment, of such words and phrases as would be likely to puzzle a student facing for the first time a bookseller's or auctioneer's catalog.

4.11 The bookman's concise dictionary. London, [1956].

Useful for British terms.

4.12 Deutsch, Babette. Poetry handbook: a dictionary of terms. Rev. ed. N.Y., [1962].

The definitions are elementary and clear. (Works on versification usually aid greatly in defining poetical terms, e.g., George R. Stewart, Jr., *The Technique of English Verse,* N.Y., [1930]; Paull F. Baum, *The Principles of English Versification,* Cambridge, Mass., 1922; 1923. For others, see 22.18, Karl Shapiro.)

4.13 Bowman, Walter P., and Ball, Robert H. Theatre language: a dictionary of terms in English of the drama and stage from medieval to modern times. N.Y., [1961].

Over 3,000 terms and phrases, including recent jargon, cant, and slang.

See also 35.9-14.

5. PREPARATION OF MANUSCRIPTS FOR PUBLICATION

5.1   On the publication of research: essays by R. B. McKerrow and Henry M. Silver. Reprinted from PMLA, v. 65 (April, 1950). N.Y., [1950].
Brief practical instructions on how to organize an article, how to prepare the MS, and principles to follow in reading proof.

5.2   The MLA style sheet. Comp. William R. Parker. Rev. ed. N.Y., [1961].
Directions for preparing MSS, footnotes, and bibliographies for theses. The style suggested here is used by a large number of scholarly journals. (The pamphlet may be obtained from the Modern Language Association of America, 6 Washington Square North, N.Y. 3.)

5.3   A manual of style. By the staff of the University of Chicago press. 11th rev. ed. Chicago, 1949.
Rules for preparation of copy, suggestions for editing, glossaries of technical terms, specimens of type, etc. This work is widely used by magazine and book publishers.

5.4   Von Ostermann, Georg F. Manual of foreign languages. 4th ed. rev. N.Y., 1952.
Editorial manual indicating peculiarities of capitalization, accents, abbreviations, numerals, etc. for a large and diverse list of languages.

5.5   Nicholson, Margaret. A manual of copyright practice for writers, publishers, and agents. 2d ed. N.Y., 1956.
"What to do in a specific situation involving copyright."

5.6   Wittenberg, Philip. The law of literary property. Cleveland and N.Y., [1957].
On American laws concerning copyright, libel, permissions for quotations, censorship, etc. See also Norman H. Pearson, "Problems of Literary Executorship," *Studies in Bibliography*, v. 5, pp. 3-20 (1952-1953). *Copyright Law Symposium Number Ten*, N.Y., 1959, contains essays by law students offering advice on such matters as reproducing printed works on microfilm, the amount and kind of quotation that are legally permissible, the use of manuscripts, and an author's rights in his article published in a magazine. (The history of an important phase of copyright is dealt with by Aubert J. Clark in *The Movement for International Copyright in Nineteenth Century America*, Washington, 1960. Joseph W. Rogers, *U.S. National Bibliography and the Copyright Law*, N.Y., [1961], is chiefly a review of the history of catalogs of copyright entries since 1891.)

5.7   Spiker, Sina. Indexing your book: a practical guide for authors. Madison, Wis., 1955.

5.8   Byrd, Milton B., and Goldsmith, Arnold L. Publication guide for literary and linguistic scholars. Detroit, 1958.

Lists 180 journals, chiefly of interest to scholars in English and American literature, with subscription data, editorial policies, and information on the nature and handling of MSS.

5.9   Gerstenberger, Donna, and Hendrick, George. Directory of periodicals publishing articles in English and American literature and language. Denver, [1959].

Lists 386 periodicals with pertinent information on each. Included are several journals devoted to folklore and some "little" magazines that "carry an occasional critical article." See also 7.11.

5.10   American journals in the humanities: a guide to scope and editorial policy. Reprinted from PMLA, v. 72 (September, 1957). N.Y., [1957].

The policies of 48 periodicals. Addresses of the editorial offices and names of editors appear regularly in *PMLA*'s "Directory of Useful Addresses," appended to its annual list of members (September).

5.11   The literary market place. N.Y., 1940——.

Annual directory which arranges American publishers by location and by type of books published. It also supplies lists of national associations, literary awards, columnists, radio book programs, magazines and newspapers containing book news, etc. (Literary awards are more extensively considered in *Literary and Library Prizes*, 5th ed. N.Y., 1963.)

6. LIBRARY OF CONGRESS CATALOGS AND CHIEF REGISTERS OF U. S. PUBLICATIONS

6.1   A catalog of books represented by Library of Congress printed cards issued to July 31, 1942. 167 v. Ann Arbor, Mich., 1942-1946; Paterson, N.J., 1960.

Photographic reproduction of nearly two million cards, alphabetically arranged. Not all the books represented by the cards are in the Library of Congress. This work does not cover all the holdings of the Library of Congress—but only such works for which cards were printed, even when the works were in other libraries—from August, 1898, to 1942.

6.2   ——— Supplement: cards issued August 1, 1942—December 31, 1947. 42 v. Ann Arbor, Mich., 1948; Paterson, N.J., 1960.

6.3   The Library of Congress author catalog: a cumulative list of works represented by Library of Congress printed cards 1948-1952. 24 v. Ann Arbor, Mich., 1953; Paterson, N.J., 1960.

V. 24 lists motion pictures and film strips.

6.4   The national union catalog: a cumulative author list representing Library of Congress printed cards and titles reported by other American libraries 1953-1957. 28 v. Ann Arbor, Mich., 1958; N.Y., 1961. Supplement 1952-1955. 30 v. Ann Arbor, Mich., 1961.

The last two volumes register music, phonorecords, motion pictures, and film strips. Since 1956 includes "not only Library of Congress cards but also cards representing titles with 1956 or later imprints reported to the National Union Catalog by other North American libraries, together with locations of all such titles reported to the National Union Catalog." Continued serially as *National Union Catalog.* (The author list for 1958 has been reprinted, 5 v., N.Y., 1962.) See 1.10 for complementary subject list.

6.5   Evans, Charles. American bibliography: a chronological dictionary of all books, pamphlets and periodical publications printed in the U.S. . . . 1639- [1800]. 14 v. Chicago, and Worcester, Mass., 1903-1959.

V. 13, edited by Clifford K. Shipton, was published in Worcester, Mass. V. 14, likewise published in Worcester, is an index, prepared by Roger P. Bristol, who is also responsible for *Index of Printers, Publishers, and Booksellers Indicated by Charles Evans in His American Bibliography,* Charlottesville, Va., 1961. The earlier volumes were reprinted by Peter Smith, Gloucester, Mass., in 1941. A number of "ghost" titles appear, especially in the

earlier volumes. (The American Antiquarian Society is in process of reproducing in microprint all the available works listed in Evans.)

6.6   Waters, Willard O. American imprints, 1648-1797, in the Huntington
Library, supplementing Evans' American Bibliography. [Cambridge,
Mass., 1933].

Reprinted from *Huntington Library Bulletin,* no. 3 (February, 1933).

6.7   Stark, Lewis M., and Cole, Maud D. Checklist of additions to Evans'
American Bibliography in the rare book room of the New York
Public Library. N.Y., 1960.

6.8   Shaw, Ralph R., and Shoemaker, Richard H. American bibliography.
a preliminary checklist for 1801——. N.Y., 1958——.

Compiled entirely from secondary sources, this makes a tentative step in
filling the gap in the listing of American publications for the period 1801-1819
inclusive. The entries are uneven in quality, but the locations of copies are
included. (For this period there are also many state or regional lists of imprints.)

6.9   Growoll, Adolf. Book-trade bibliography in the U.S. in the 19th
century. N.Y., 1898; [1939].

Lists the chief older sources of information on works printed in the U.S.
during the century.

6.10   Sabin, Joseph. Bibliotheca Americana: a dictionary of books relating
to America, from its discovery. . . . 29 v. N.Y., 1868-1936; Amsterdam, 1961-1962.

Includes works published in America and about America printed elsewhere.
Arrangement is alphabetical by author, primarily. In later volumes the scope
is materially reduced. Like Evans, this often mentions libraries owning copies,
and hence is useful for interlibrary loans.

6.11   Roorbach, Orville A. Bibliotheca Americana, 1820-1861. 4 v. N.Y.,
1852-1861; 1939.

Catalog of publications, including reprints, arranged by authors and titles,
giving publisher, date, price. By no means are all American published works
of the period listed.

6.12   Kelly, James. American catalogue of books published in the U.S.
from January, 1861 to January, 1871. 2 v. N.Y., 1866-1871; 1938.

Like Roorbach, far from complete.

6.13   The American catalogue, 1876-1910. 9 v. in 13. N.Y., 1876-1910;
1941.

(For the gap between 1872 and 1876, see *Publishers' Weekly,* 1872-1876. Lee
Ash, 31 Alden Rd., New Haven 15, Conn., is planning a cumulative index
for this period.)

6.14   Annual American catalogue, 1869-1872, 1886-1910. 25 v. N.Y.,
1887-1911.

Inferior to, but sometimes supplementary to, *American Catalogue.*

6.15   The United States catalog: books in print.   Minneapolis and N.Y., 1900——.

Since 1928 lists also certain publications in English outside the U.S.

6.16   Cumulative book index.   N.Y., 1898——.

Periodically issued to form supplements to *United States Catalog.*

6.17   Publishers' weekly, 1872——.   N.Y., 1872——.

Lists new publications weekly.   Books are often announced in advance, in special numbers issued in January (for spring), May (for summer), and September (for fall).

6.18   American Book Publishing Record.   February, 1960——.

Cumulates monthly the *Publishers' Weekly* announcements, along with full Library of Congress cataloging.

6.19   Books in print: an author-title-series index to the Publishers' Trade List Annual.   N.Y., 1948——.

Registers by authors and then by titles all the books listed for sale in the current catalogs of the vast majority of American publishers.   (For the corresponding subject index, see 1.12.)

6.20   Paperbound books in print.   N.Y., 1955——.

Serially issued by the R. R. Bowker Co.   Indexed by subject, author, and title.   American publishers only.

7. INDEXES TO CONTENTS OF MAGAZINES

7.1   Poole's index to periodical literature, 1802-1907. 7 v. in 6. N.Y., 1938.
Subject index only.

7.2   Cushing, Helen G., and Morris, Adah V. Nineteenth century readers' guide to periodical literature, 1890-1899: with supplementary indexing 1900-1922. 2 v. N.Y., 1944.
Fifty-one British and American magazines are covered for the nineties, and fourteen are continued beyond 1899. Many anonymous contributors are identified.

7.3   Readers' guide to periodical literature, 1900———. Minneapolis, etc., 1905———.

7.4   International index to periodicals, devoted chiefly to the humanities and science, 1907———. N.Y., etc., 1916———.

7.5   Annual magazine subject index, 1907-1949. 43 v. Boston, 1908-1952.
About half of the magazines covered relate to history, especially American local history. Also contains "Dramatic Index" of books and articles on drama and theater.

7.6   The book review digest, 1905———. N.Y., 1906———.
Excerpts from the early reviews of selected newly published books. The periodicals covered are largely general organs like weeklies that review books fairly soon after they appear. Helpful in obtaining a cursory view of contents of books and a sampling of the reviewers' reactions to them.

7.7   Index to little magazines, 1948———. Denver, 1949———.
Sporadic publication, for the most part annual. Covers primarily literary contents of selected "little" magazines which are not indexed in *Readers' Guide* or *International Index*.

7.8   Index to early American periodical literature, 1728-1870. N.Y., 1941.
Describes a card index, compiled by WPA, housed at New York University and available for the use of scholars.

7.9   O'Neill, Edward H.   A description and an analysis of the bibliography of American literature.   Philadelphia, 1941.

Describes a card index, compiled by WPA, housed at the University of Pennsylvania and available for the use of scholars.   Like the N.Y.U. index, this is very useful in making lists of works by minor authors published in older American periodicals.

7.10   Haskell, Daniel C.   A checklist of cumulative indexes to individual periodicals in the New York Public Library.   N.Y., 1942.

Helps to answer questions like, "Is there a published index to the contents of the *Atlantic Monthly?*"

7.11   Ulrich's periodical directory: a classified guide to a selected list of current periodicals, foreign and domestic.   Ed. Eileen C. Graves.   10th ed. N.Y., 1963.

Tells where the periodicals are indexed and brings Haskell up to date for cumulative indexes of individual magazines.

7.12   Abstracts of English studies.   1958———.

Monthly publication abstracting articles in a variety of professional journals of interest to students of English and American literature and the English language.

7.13   An index to book reviews in the humanities.   V. 1 ——— March 13, 1960———.

A quarterly covering certain newspapers as well as selected magazines.

8. AMERICAN STUDIES OR AMERICAN CIVILIZATION

8.1   Mugridge, Donald H., and McCrum, Blanche P.   A guide to the study of the U. S. of America: representative books reflecting the development of American life and thought.   Washington, 1960.

The largest and most diversified annotated list of books concerned with the several aspects of American "civilization," this excellent compilation was supervised by Roy P. Basler.   Coverage to 1955.   Among the contents are entries on literature (pp. 1-175), literary history and criticism (pp. 183-223), periodicals and journalism (pp. 244-268), general history, diplomatic history, and foreign relations (pp. 300-438), science and technology (pp. 625-647), entertainment (pp. 672-684), sports and recreation (pp. 685-700), education (pp. 701-724), philosophy and psychology (pp. 725-751), religion (pp. 752-784), folklore, folk music, folk art (pp. 785-815), music (pp. 816-840), art and architecture (pp. 841-872), economic life (pp. 893-948), constitution and government (pp. 949-997), and books and libraries (pp. 1062-1080). The annotations vary in quality and were made chiefly by librarians.   A ten-year supplement is planned to pick up from 1955.

8.2   American quarterly.   1949———.

Official organ of the American Studies Association.   A supplementary issue lists annually dissertations in progress in the field of American Studies, articles of an interdisciplinary sort, and works on the theory and teaching of American Civilization.   The ASA also issues *American Studies,* primarily a pedagogical newsletter.

8.3   Carman, Harry J., and Thompson, Arthur W.   A guide to the principal sources for American civilization, 1800-1900, in the city of New York.   2 v.   Manuscripts.   N. Y., 1960.   Printed materials. N. Y., 1962.

Of far greater use than the limitation to one city might suggest.   A kind of predecessor is Evarts B. Greene and Richard B. Morris, *A Guide to the Principal Sources for Early American History (1600-1800) in the City of New York,* 2d ed., N. Y., 1953.

8.4   Crick, B. R., and Alman, Miriam, eds.   A guide to manuscripts relating to America in Great Britain and Ireland.   London, 1961.

Manuscripts, letters, etc. of authors are also included.   See also Crick's article, "A Survey of Library Resources in the United Kingdom for the Teaching of American History and Literature in the Universities," *Journal of Documentation,* v. 14, pp. 109-118 (1958).

8.5   Walker, Robert H. American studies in the U.S.: a survey of college programs. Baton Rouge, La., [1958].

Provides information on the various American Studies programs and discusses the movement as a whole; contains bibliography.

8.6   American literature in the college curriculum. By a committee on the college study of American literature and culture of the National Council of Teachers of English. Chicago, 1948.

Analysis of courses in the subject offered in 1946 and a study of the growth of American Civilization programs.

8.7   Bowden, Edwin T., ed. American studies: problems, promises and possibilities. Austin, Texas, 1958.

A panel discussion which deals informally with a number of general matters, particularly the organization of courses.

8.8   Kwiat, Joseph T., and Turpie, M. C., eds. Studies in American culture: dominant ideas and images. Minneapolis, 1960.

Includes several essays, by various hands, on methodology, including a reprint of the following item.

8.9   Smith, Henry N. "Can 'American Studies' develop a method?" American quarterly, v. 9, pp. 197-208 (Summer, 1957).

8.10   Skard, Sigmund. American studies in Europe: their history and present organization. 2 v. Philadelphia, [1958].

Describes seminars, institutes, and programs concerned with the U.S. in various European countries. Also contains much information on the reception of American literature in Europe in days gone by. Skard's *The American Myth and the European Mind: American Studies in Europe 1776-1960*, Philadelphia, [1961], is a semi-popular redaction of the above which only occasionally comes closer to date.

8.11   Newsletter of the European Association for American Studies. 1955——.

Includes a current bibliography. The Association was founded in 1954 at a meeting in Salzburg. The British Association for American Studies (founded 1955) also publishes a *Bulletin* (1956——). The Nordic Association for American Studies (founded 1959) likewise engages in publication.

8.12   Jahrbuch für Amerikastudien. Heidelberg, 1956——.

Official annual of the German Society for American Studies, chiefly devoted to articles, some in English, on literature and history. Contains also reviews, bibliographies, and lists of dissertations. The German SAS also issues a *Mitteilungsblatt*, which contains bibliography and lists of dissertations, as well as information about the activities of the various institutes and seminars concerned with American Studies. (German dissertations on English and American literature are periodically listed also in *Zeitschrift für Anglistik und Amerikanistik*, 1953——, published in East Germany.)

8.13   Studi Americani. Rome, 1955——.

An annual devoted to the literature and art of the U.S. Some of the articles are in English.

9. AMERICAN HISTORY: GENERAL TOOLS

9.1 Harvard guide to American history. Ed. Oscar Handlin *et al.* Cambridge, Mass., 1954.

Extensive lists of works on all phases of the subject, clearly arranged and well indexed. Coverage to 1951. Preliminary chapters deal with the nature of the historian's task and preparation for research and writing.

9.2 Beers, Henry P. Bibliographies in American history: guide to materials for research. 2d ed. N.Y., 1942; Paterson, N.J., 1959.

Often outmoded by the *Harvard Guide,* but still useful because of its independent index and arrangement. *The American Historical Association's Guide to Historical Literature,* ed. George F. Howe *et al,* N. Y., 1961, of course includes selected works on all aspects of American history, pp. 711-744.

9.3 Writings on American history, 1902———. 1904———.

A series of volumes, published annually, with a few gaps, containing a list of books and important articles on all phases of American history. Some of the earlier volumes are available in reprints, N. Y., 1962. See item immediately following.

9.4 Index to the writings on American history 1902-1940. Compiled for the American Historical Association. Washington, [1956].

Contains references and subject classifications not to be found in the separate indexes of the annual volumes.

9.5 American historical review. 1895———.

Official organ of the American Historical Association; largely devoted to current bibliography and reviews of books, including extensive lists of current books and articles on the history of the U.S. and its various sections.

9.6 Mississippi Valley historical review. 1914———.

The chief journal devoted solely to American history; essays, book reviews, bibliographical notices, and check lists of articles, the last not so inclusive as similar lists in *American Historical Review.*

9.7 List of doctoral dissertations in history in progress or completed at colleges and universities in the U.S. since 1958. Washington, 1961.

This list is now published triennially by the American Historical Association. The 1955 listing included only dissertations in progress.

9.8   Billington, Ray A.   Guides to American history manuscript collections in libraries of the U.S.   N.Y., 1952.

Reprinted from *Mississippi Valley Historical Review*, v. 38, no. 3 (December, 1951).   Cf. also the lists of guides to manuscript materials in *Harvard Guide*, 9.1, pp. 79-88, Hamer, 1.14, Crick and Alman, 8.4, and Carman and Thompson, 8.3.

9.9   Morris, Richard B., and Commager, Henry S., eds.   The new American nation series.   N. Y., 1954————.

An extensive history covering the whole range of American history and planned for 43 volumes.   Each volume is written by an authority who also supplies a critical bibliography.   (In progress also is the Chicago History of American Civilization, ed. Daniel J. Boorstin, Chicago, 1956————, planned to include 20 volumes, of slighter compass and with less extensive bibliographies.)

9.10   Morison, Samuel E., and Commager, Henry S.   The growth of the American republic.   5th ed.   2 v.   N.Y., 1962.

One of the most widely used basic textbooks.

9.11   Schlesinger, Arthur M., and Fox, Dixon R., eds.   A history of American life.   13 v.   N.Y., 1927-1948.

The most extensive social history of the U.S.   The individual volumes, written by various authors, are uneven in quality and coverage.   Contains critically annotated bibliographies for all chapters.

9.12   Adams, James T., ed.   Dictionary of American history.   5 v. plus index.   2d rev. ed.   N.Y., 1946.   Supplement One.   Ed. J. G. E. Hopkins and Wayne Andrews.   N.Y., 1961.

Contains no biographical sketches.   The supplement extends or revises older entries and extends coverage 1940-1960.

9.13   Morris, Richard B., ed.   Encyclopedia of American history.   **Rev. ed.** N.Y., [1961].

A basic chronology is followed by a topical outline, plus biographical data on 300 notable Americans.   One of the best chronological outlines of American "Civilization."

9.14   Carruth, Gorton, *et al.*, eds. The encyclopedia of American facts and dates.   3d ed.   N.Y., [1962].

Includes listings through 1961 and is very fully indexed.

9.15   The pageant of America: a pictorial history of the U.S.   Ed. **Ralph** H. Gabriel *et al.*   15 v.   [New Haven, Conn., 1925-1929].

The most extensive pictorial survey, from Indians to football.

9.16   Adams, James T., *et al*, eds.   Album of American history.   5 v.   N.Y., 1944-1960.

Pictures illustrating the social history of the U.S. from Colonial times to 1953.   (For other pictorial records see *Harvard Guide* 9.1, pp. 64-68.)

9.17   Historical statistics of the U.S. colonial times to 1957.   Prepared by the Bureau of the Census with the co-operation of the Social Science Research Council.   [Washington], [1960].

For more recent data, including revisions, see *Statistical Abstract of the U.S.*, Washington, 1957————.

9.18 Paullin, Charles O. Atlas of the historical geography of the U.S. Ed. John K. Wright. [Washington and N.Y.], 1932.

Other atlases of considerable breadth include Clifford L. Lord and Elizabeth H. Lord, *Historical Atlas of the United States*, rev. ed., N.Y., 1953, and James T. Adams and Roy V. Coleman, *Atlas of American History*, N.Y., [1943].

9.19 Peterson, Clarence S. Consolidated bibliography of county histories in fifty states in 1961, consolidated 1935-1961. Baltimore, 1961.

Privately reproduced by the compiler, this aims to list "all county histories of at least 100 pages, with few exceptions."

9.20 Directory of historical societies and agencies in the U.S. and Canada 1956. Columbus, Ohio, 1956.

Names, addresses, and titles of officers to whom correspondence should be addressed.

9.21 Crittenden, Christopher, and Godard, Doris. Historical societies in the U.S. and Canada. Washington, 1944.

Mentions their publications, general contents of their libraries and collections, etc.

9.22 Theory and practice in historical study: a report of the committee on historiography. Social Science Research Council bulletin, no. 54. N.Y., [1946].

Chapter 2 discusses "Controlling Assumptions in the Practice of American Historians," and Chapter 6 is "Selective Reading List on Historiography and the Philosophy of History," including most of the important works by Americans. Cf. also 2.2, Howe *et al.*

9.23 Wish, Harvey. The American historian: a social-intellectual history of the writing of the American past. N.Y., 1960.

After two preliminary chapters the discussion centers on Sparks, Hildreth, Bancroft, Parkman, McMaster, Henry Adams, Turner, Von Holst, Phillips, Beard, Parrington, and Nevins. Bibliographical notes appear.

9.24 Kraus, Michael. The writing of American history. Norman, Okla., [1953].

A pioneer work on American historiography.

9.25 Hutchinson, William T., ed. The Marcus W. Jernegan essays in American historiography. Chicago, [1937]; [N.Y., 1958].

Twenty-one historians of Americana are treated by various authors.

9.26 Van Tassel, David D. Recording America's past: an interpretation of the development of historical studies in America 1607-1884. Chicago, 1960.

A grass-roots approach to causes and trends which throws light upon many lesser-known historians and on the development of several historical societies.

9.27 Levin, David. History as romantic art: Bancroft, Prescott, Motley, and Parkman. Stanford, Calif., 1959.

Disjointed but often excellent analysis of the art and background ideas of the four historians.

9.28   Benson, Lee. Turner and Beard: American historical writing recon-
sidered. Glencoe, Ill., 1960.

Finds more in common between the two historians than one had ever
imagined.

H. A. IRONSIDE MEMORIAL LIBRARY

10. AMERICAN HISTORY: SOME SPECIAL STUDIES

10.1   Andrews, Charles M.   The Colonial period of American history.   4 v.   New Haven, Conn., 1934-1938.

10.2   Nye, Russel B.   The cultural life of the new nation 1776-1830.   N.Y., [1960]; [1963].

Compact, with excellent bibliography, this work is especially valuable for the student of literature.   One chapter deals with "The Quest for a National Literature."

10.3   A history of the South.   Ed. Wendell H. Stephenson and E. Merton Coulter.   10 v. planned.   [Baton Rouge, La.], 1947——.

Various authorities cover the region from 1607 to 1913.

10.4   Bernard, Luther L., and Bernard, Jessie.   Origins of American sociology: the social science movement in the U.S.   N.Y., [1943].

History of social-science theory in the 19th century.

10.5   David, Henry, *et al.,* eds.   The economic history of the U.S.   9 v.   N.Y., 1945——.

Various excellent authorities detail economic development from Colonial times to 1941.

10.6   Kelly, Alfred H., and Harbison, Winfred A.   The American constitution, its origins and development.   Rev. ed.   N.Y., [1955].

The Constitution itself, annotated with cases decided by the Supreme Court to June 30, 1952, may be found in 82 Congress, 2 Session, Senate Documents, no. 170, Washington, 1953, ed. Edward S. Corwin.   Dorothy C. Tompkins, *The Supreme Court of the U.S.,* Berkeley, Calif., 1959, is an annotated bibliography useful for the history of the court, its *modus operandi,* and its relationship to the other branches of the government.

10.7   Binkley, Wilfred E.   American political parties, their natural history.   4th ed. rev.   N.Y., 1962.

A standard textbook which includes bibliography.   Ranging outside the discussion of political parties and elections is *Politics, Parties and Pressure Groups,* by Valdimer O. Key, 4th ed., N.Y., [1958].

10.8   Jones, Maldwyn A.   American immigration.   Chicago, 1960.

Compactly reassembles the long-established facts along with recent scholarship and includes bibliographical comments which serve as a handy guide.

10.9   Wittke, Carl F.   We who built America: the saga of the immigrant. N.Y., 1939; 1940.

Broader outlines of the entire history of immigration, plus special sections on various national groups: Irish, Germans, Orientals, Mexicans, etc.

10.10   Hansen, Marcus L.   The Atlantic migration 1607-1860.   Cambridge, Mass., 1940; N.Y., [1961].

Deals with immigration from Europe.

10.11   Bowers, David F., ed.   Foreign influences in American life: essays and critical bibliographies.   Princeton, N.J., 1944; Gloucester, Mass., 1952.

A symposium, with a cursory chapter on "The American Literary Expatriate." The bibliographies cover immigration, the pattern of assimilation, the economic impact, the political impact, the artistic and literary impact, and the religious and philosophic impact.

10.12   Jaffe, Bernard.   Men of science in America.   Rev. ed.   N.Y., 1958.

Semi-popular, biographical treatment.

10.13   de Camp, L. Sprague.   The heroic age of American invention.   Garden City, N.Y., 1961.

A popular treatment of Stevens, Morse, Colt, McCormick, Ericcson, Mergenthaler, Bell, Edison, Selden, the Wright brothers, *et al.*

10.14   Bode, Carl.   The American lyceum: town meeting of the mind.   N.Y., 1956.

A history of the lyceum movement.

10.15   Taylor, George R., ed.   The Turner thesis concerning the role of the frontier in American history.   Rev. ed.   Boston, [1956].

Two essays by Frederick Jackson Turner are followed by discussions pro and con, in a volume included in the series *Problems in American Civilization,* edited from Amherst College. Turner has been a vital influence on historical studies of a wide variety, including literary history. Cf. 29.9, Lucy L. Hazard.

10.16   Parry, Albert.   Garrets and pretenders: a history of Bohemianism in America.   Rev. ed.   N.Y., [1961].

A popular but incomplete account. The revision consists largely of a new chapter, on the Beatniks, by Harry T. Moore.

10.17   Filler, Louis.   Crusaders for American liberalism.   N.Y., [1939]; Yellow Springs, Ohio, [1950]; [1961].

History of the muckraking movement 1900-1915.

10.18   Butts, R. Freeman, and Cremin, Lawrence A.   A history of education in American culture.   N.Y., [1953].

10.19   Cremin, Lawrence A.   The transformation of the school: progressivism in American education, 1876-1957.   N.Y., 1961.

Puts the progressive movement in the schools in the broader context of the times.

10.20 Rudolph, Frederick. The American college and university: a history. N.Y., 1962.

A semi-popular history, with excellent footnotes and an annotated bibliography.

10.21 Berelson, Bernard. Graduate education in the U.S. N.Y., 1960.

Contains a brief history, with bibliography, and an extensive analysis of contemporary practices and problems, plus concrete recommendations for improvements in the Ph.D. system.

10.22 Schmidt, George P. The liberal arts college: a chapter in American cultural history. New Brunswick, N.J., 1957.

10.23 Flexner, Eleanor. Century of struggle: the woman's rights movement in the U.S. Cambridge, Mass., 1959.

A readable but scholarly and comprehensive account.

10.24 Spear, Dorothy N. Bibliography of American directories through 1860. Worcester, Mass., 1961.

Contains 1,647 items, of which the American Antiquarian Society holds 1,110.

11. BIOGRAPHY

11.1 Hyamson, Albert W. A dictionary of universal biography of all ages and of all peoples. 2d ed. N.Y., 1951.

An index of names included in the chief general biographical dictionaries in English and several other European languages.

11.2 Riches, Phyllis M. An analytical bibliography of universal collected biography, comprising books published in the English tongue in Great Britain and Ireland, America and the British dominions. London, 1934.

11.3 Biography index: a cumulative index to biographical material in books and magazines. N.Y., 1946——.

Quarterly index covering books and 1500 periodicals in English, chiefly American; includes obituaries and some fictional treatments.

11.4 The new Century cyclopedia of names. Ed. Clarence L. Barnhart *et al.* 3 v. N.Y., [1954].

A standard reference work for names of consequence of various nationalities.

11.5 Dictionary of American biography. 20 v. plus index, plus supplement (1944). N.Y., 1928-1937; 1946. 2d supplement, 1958.

Each sketch is followed by a list of sources, often including MS material. The following sometimes offer sketches of individuals not represented in the DAB: *Appleton's Cyclopaedia of American Biography,* 7 v., N.Y., 1887-1900 (v. 8, 1918, is an index); *Lamb's Biographical Dictionary of the U.S.,* 7 v., Boston, 1900-1903; *The National Cyclopaedia of American Biography,* 35 v., N.Y., 1892-1949 (in progress); *White's Conspectus of American Biography,* 2d ed., N.Y., 1937. (For series of more specialized biographies, see *Harvard Guide,* 9.1, pp. 188 ff.) Cf. also Jane Kline, *Biographical Sources for the U.S.,* Washington, 1961.

11.6 O'Neill, Edward H. Biography by Americans 1658-1936: a subject bibliography. Philadelphia, 1939.

A check list of biographies individual and collective written by Americans. In the cases of particularly famous men only the "important books" on them are recorded.

11.7 Dargan, Marion. Guide to American biography. Part 1, 1607-1815; part 2, 1815-1933. Albuquerque, N. Mex., 1949-1952.

Selective; arranged by chronological periods, subdivided by geographical regions.

11.8   Kaplan, Louis, *et al.* A bibliography of American autobiographies. Madison, Wis., 1961.

Coverage to 1946. A subject index classifies the books according to occupation, place of residence, and connection with historical events of the subjects. For each item one library owning a copy is indicated. See also Mary S. Carlock, "American Autobiographies, 1840-1870. a Bibliography," *Bulletin of Bibliography,* v. 23, pp. 118-120 (May-August, 1961).

11.9   Lillard, Richard G. American life in autobiography: a descriptive guide. Stanford, Calif., [1956].

Selected autobiographies are listed under headings made according to the profession or occupation of the writers, e.g., "Actors and Show People," "Journalists, Newspaper and Magazine Editors."

11.10   Matthews, William. American diaries. Berkeley and Los Angeles, 1945; Boston, 1959.

List of published diaries written prior to 1861.

11.11   Kunitz, Stanley J., and Haycraft, Howard, eds. American authors, 1600-1900. N.Y., 1938.

Contains 1300 biographical sketches and 400 portraits.

11.12   Adams, Oscar F. A dictionary of American authors. 5th ed. rev. and enlarged. Boston, 1905.

11.13   Burke, W. J., and Howe, Will D. American authors and books 1640 to the present day. Augmented and rev. by Irving Weiss. N.Y., [1962].

Brief sketches; lists many very minor names.

11.14   Herzberg, Max J., ed. The reader's encyclopedia of American literature. N.Y., [1962].

An elaborate but erratic compilation occasionally useful chiefly for sketches of minor authors available nowhere else.

11.15   Duyckinck, Evert A., and Duyckinck, George L. Cyclopaedia of American literature. Rev. ed. 2 v. Philadelphia, 1875.

Useful only for minor earlier writers.

11.16   Wallace, W. Stewart. A dictionary of North American authors deceased before 1950. Toronto, [1951].

The authors may be journalists, lawyers, merchants, etc., but many literary men are listed, by field of interest, with places and dates of birth and death.

11.17   Kunitz, Stanley J., and Haycraft, Howard. Twentieth century authors. N.Y., 1942. First supplement. N.Y., 1955.

Biographical sketches of 1850 authors of various nationalities, but chiefly American, plus 1700 portraits. The supplement adds about 700 new authors, usually those who have come into prominence since 1942.

11.18   Who's who in America. Chicago, 1899———.

Biennial publication containing sketches of living individuals, who themselves supply the information. (For persons dropped because of death there is a *Who Was Who*. *Who's Who in the East* and other sectional compilations include many additional names. *Who's Who of American Women*, 1958-1959, began another series.)

11.19   Contemporary authors. March, 1962———.

Quarterly information service on current authors, chiefly American.

11.20   O'Neill, Edward H.   A history of American biography, 1800-1935. Philadelphia, 1935.

11.21   Directory of American scholars, a biographical directory.   Ed. Jaques Cattell.   3d ed.   N.Y., 1957.

Historians and scholars in the various fields of literature and the humanities. A 4th edition, in 4 v., is in preparation, N.Y., 1963———.

11.22   Doane, Gilbert H.   Searching for your ancestors.   [3d ed.]   Minneapolis, [1960].

A guide to genealogical investigation.   Methodology of genealogical research is considered also in George B. Everton, Sr., and Gunnar Rasmuson, *The Handy Book for Genealogists*, 3d ed., Logan, Utah, [1957]; Archibald F. Bennett, *A Guide for Genealogical Research*, Salt Lake City, 1951; and Jacques Barzun and Henry F. Graff, *The Modern Researcher*, N.Y., [1957]; [1963].

11.23   The American genealogical-biographical index to American genealogical, biographical and local history materials.   Middletown, Conn., 1952———.

The first 41 v. cover names Aabrey through Deerin.

See also 3.12-13, 13.1, 19.7-8, 19.36, 19.51-53, and 21.16 *(Oxford Companion to American Literature)*.

12. MAGAZINES

12.1   Ditzion, Sidney. "The history of periodical literature in the U.S.: a bibliography." Bulletin of bibliography, v. 15, pp. 110, 129-133 (1935).

Incomplete and out of date, but occasionally useful. (Cf. bibliographies in section on Newspapers.)

12.2   Gregory, Winifred. Union list of serials in libraries of the U.S. and Canada. 2d ed. N.Y., 1943.

A vastly expanded third edition, ed. Edna B. Titus, is shortly to be published—with 157,000 titles held by 835 libraries. This standard work locates files of magazines of all sorts. Many new files appear in supplements, published 1945 and 1953. For serials which commenced publication since 1949, see *New Serial Titles,* issued by the Library of Congress, 1956——. (American magazines 1741-1850 have been, or are in process of being, made available on microfilm, through University Microfilms, Inc., Ann Arbor, Mich. For annual lists of magazines, with circulation figures, see the N. W. Ayer annual, 13.9.)

12.3   Mott, Frank L. A history of American magazines. V. 1, 1741-1850; v. 2, 1850-1865; v. 3, 1865-1885; v. 4, 1885-1905. Cambridge, Mass., 1938-1957.

The standard work in its field. Various aspects of magazine journalism are discussed as a part of the social history of the times. Certain periodicals important in the period covered in a volume are given extended historical treatment in a supplementary section, and when such publications extend beyond the chronological limits of a volume, they are carried forward to their ends or to the date of publication of the volume. For example, in v. 4 the histories of the *Saturday Evening Post, Ladies Home Journal,* and *National Geographic* are carried down to 1957. (Mr. Mott is at work on v. 5.)

12.4   Tassin, Algernon. The magazine in America. N.Y., 1916.

Informal and out of date, but still probably the best of the single-volume histories for the use of students of literature.

12.5   Wood, James P. Magazines in the U.S. 2d ed. N.Y., [1956].

Suggestive for the period not as yet treated by Mott.

12.6   Peterson, Theodore. Magazines in the twentieth century. Urbana, Ill., 1956.

Covers American magazines of general circulation, with special emphasis on the advertising-production-circulation complex.

12.7 Richardson, Lyon N. A history of early American magazines, 1741-1789. N.Y., 1931.

(All known magazines of the 18th century published in the U.S. have been made available on microfilm through University Microfilms, Inc., Ann Arbor, Mich.)

12.8 Lewis, Benjamin M. A register of editors, printers, and publishers of American magazines, 1741-1810. N.Y., 1957.

12.9 Lewis, Benjamin M. An introduction to American magazines, 1800-1810. Ann Arbor, Mich., 1961.

Covers 130 magazines published during the decade.

12.10 Smyth, Albert H. The Philadelphia magazines and their contributors, 1741-1850. Philadelphia, 1892.

12.11 Fleming, Herbert E. Magazines of a market-metropolis: being a history of the literary periodicals and literary interests of Chicago. Chicago, 1906.

Originally published in *American Journal of Sociology*, v. 11 and 12.

12.12 Gilmer, Gertrude C. Checklist of Southern periodicals to 1861. Boston, 1934.

12.13 Gohdes, Clarence. The periodicals of American transcendentalism. Durham, N. C., 1931.

Historical account of various magazines of the 19th century conducted by people who were identified with the Transcendentalists—Emerson, Theodore Parker, *et al.*

12.14 Noel, Mary. Villains galore. N.Y., 1954.

History of popular 19th-century story weeklies like the N.Y. *Ledger*.

12.15 Ulrich, Carolyn, and Patterson, Eugenia. Little magazines: a list. N.Y., 1947.

Includes the periodicals in the N.Y. Public Library; period covered 1890-1946.

12.16 Union list of little magazines. Chicago, 1956.

A list of 1,037 little magazines in libraries of various Middle-Western universities, compiled under the auspices of Indiana University Library.

12.17 Hoffman, Frederick J., *et al.* The little magazine: a history and a bibliography. [2d ed.] Princeton, N.J., 1947.

Partially supplemented by J. B. May, *Twigs as Varied Bent*, Corona, N.Y., 1954. Since 1952 the magazine *Trace* has reported the births and deaths of many little magazines and put out an annual *International Guide*, London, 1960——, by no means exhaustive.

13. NEWSPAPERS

13.1 Price, Warren C. The literature of journalism: an annotated bibliography. Minneapolis, [1959].

Centered principally on the U.S. and Canada, this book lists histories of journalism and of individual newspapers and magazines, biographies of editors and journalists, and works on kindred subjects, including radio and television. "The base of the work is frankly historical and biographical."

13.2 Cannon, Carl L. Journalism: a bibliography. [N.Y.], 1924.

Chiefly works in English on various aspects of newspaperdom, primarily of the U.S.

13.3 Wolseley, Roland E. The journalist's book shelf: an annotated and selected bibliography of U.S. journalism. 7th ed. Chicago, 1961.

Begun in 1939 as a supplement to Cannon. Contains helpful lists of biographies of journalists and works on magazines as well as newspapers and the craft of writing for them.

13.4 Journalism quarterly. 1924———.

Since 1930 includes annotated bibliographies on various journalistic subjects.

13.5 Editor & publisher international yearbook. N.Y., 1920———.

Includes since 1936 a selective bibliography on journalistic matters.

13.6 Gregory, Winifred. American newspapers 1821-1936, a union list of files available in the U.S. and Canada. N.Y., 1937.

Rapidly being superseded by the numerous union lists covering newspaper files located in various cities, states, or regions.

13.7 Downs, Robert B., et al. American library resources: a bibliographical guide. Chicago, 1951. Supplement, 1950-1961. Chicago, 1962.

Lists, among other materials, a limited number of published check lists of local holdings of newspapers and magazines. (There are numerous catalogs of newspapers of various states and localities as well as of holdings of individual libraries. Consult the card catalog of your library under the name of state, locality, or special library.)

13.8 Newspapers on microfilm. 4th ed. Washington, 1961.

Chiefly American papers are listed, with the years for which microfilm has been made. Acknowledged to be incomplete. Additional reports of microfilmed newspapers appear in *Microfilming Clearing House Bulletin,* an occasional appendix to the Library of Congress, *Information Bulletin*. Microphoto Inc. of Cleveland, Ohio, also issues *Newspapers on Microfilm*, 7th ed., 1961-1962, which is occasionally useful.

13.9   N. W. Ayer & Son's directory of newspapers and periodicals. Philadelphia, 1880——.

Lists annually, by state and city, newspapers and certain other periodicals published in the U.S. and Canada and supplies relevant information, including circulation, political affiliation, etc.

13.10   Rowell's American newspaper directory . . . 1869-1908. Ed. George P. Presbury. 40 v. in 61. N.Y., 1869-1908.

A list of papers and periodicals, with circulation figures, etc., long a rival of N. W. Ayer & Son's annual and in 1908 merged with it.

13.11   Mott, Frank L. American journalism: a history, 1690-1960. 3d ed. N.Y., [1962].

Standard work on the history of American newspapers.

13.12   Emery, Edwin, and Smith, Henry L. The press and America. 2d ed. rev. N.Y., 1963.

A comprehensive history plus an examination of current activities in the world of papers, magazines, radio, television, and newsgathering.

13.13   Rosewater, Victor. History of coöperative news-gathering in the U.S. N.Y., 1930.

13.14   Watson, Elmo S. A history of newspaper syndicates in the U.S., 1865-1935. Chicago, 1936.

13.15   Brigham, Clarence S. History and bibliography of American newspapers 1690-1820. 2 v. Worcester, Mass., 1947; Hamden, Conn., 1962.

The standard work for its period. The reprint includes also "Additions and Corrections to History and Bibliography of American Newspapers, 1690-1820," *Proceedings of the American Antiquarian Society*, v. 71, pp. 15-62 (1961).

13.16   Schlesinger, Arthur M. Prelude to independence: the newspaper war on Britain 1764-1776. N.Y., 1958.

Contains much material on several papers of the times, including an appendix on their circulations.

13.17   Brayer, Herbert O. "Preliminary guide to indexed newspapers in the U.S., 1850-1900." Mississippi Valley historical review, v. 33, pp. 237-258 (September, 1946).

The indexes are often on cards. Repositories are indicated. Very incomplete.

13.18   Kobre, Sidney. Modern American journalism. Tallahassee, Fla., 1959.

An attempt to tell the story from 1900 in terms of sociological interaction and internal policies.

13.19 New-York Daily Tribune index for 1875-1906. 31 v. N.Y., 1876-[1907].

13.20 The New York Times index. N.Y., 1913———.

There is also available a microfilm index of the contents of the *Times,* 1851-1905; 1905-1912 is in process of being filmed.

13.21 The Wall Street Journal index. N.Y., December, 1957———.

Appears monthly, with yearly accumulations; based on the N.Y. edition.

13.22 Press intelligence directory: a manual of newspaper content, local writers, and syndicated columnists. Washington, [1957].

Part II is a list of topics—e.g., book news, theater news—followed by selected examples of papers carrying such material and often supplying names of the local writers of it.

13.23 Detweiler, Frederick G. The Negro press in the U.S. Chicago, [1922].

13.24 Arndt, Karl J. German-American newspapers and periodicals, 1732-1955: history and bibliography. Heidelberg, 1961.

14. BOOK TRADE AND PUBLISHING

14.1   Lehmann-Haupt, Hellmut, *et al.* The book in America: a history of the making and selling of books in the U.S. 2d ed. N.Y., 1951; 1952.
The standard work on its subject. Some recent books on publishing are to be found in Eleanor Blum, *Reference Books in the Mass Media: An Annotated Selected Booklist Covering Book Publishing, Broadcasting, Films, Newspapers, Magazines, and Advertising*, Urbana, Ill., 1962.

14.2   Thomas, Isaiah. The history of printing in America. 2d ed. 2 v. Albany, 1874.
Long out of date, but contains certain information not available elsewhere.

14.3   McMurtrie, Douglas C. A history of printing in the U.S.: Middle and South Atlantic States. N.Y., 1936.
Covers Pennsylvania, Maryland, New York, New Jersey, Delaware, District of Columbia, Virginia, South Carolina, North Carolina, and Georgia to 1800. (McMurtrie also edited a vast assortment of bibliographies listing the early imprints of various states and sections.) Lawrence C. Wroth, *The Colonial Printer*, 2d ed., Portland, Me., 1938, surveys the presses of the Colonies to 1800.

14.4   Bowker lectures on book publishing. [Collected ed.] N.Y., 1957.
A reprint of the first 17 Bowker lectures, 1935-1956. A new lecture is given each year and is separately published.

14.5   Stern, Madeleine B. Imprints on history: book publishers and American frontiers. Bloomington, Ind., 1956.
Chiefly concerned with various regional publishers but contains also a list of 191 firms surviving from the era prior to 1900. Walter Sutton, *The Western Book Trade*, Columbus, Ohio, 1961, views Cincinnati as a publishing and book-selling center during the 19th century.

14.6   Charvat, William. Literary publishing in America, 1790-1850. Philadelphia, 1959.
A "skimming" and a condensation of materials collected on the subject of the history of the economics of authorship. Of considerable value in explaining the careers of various prominent authors.

14.7   Shove, Raymond H. Cheap book production in the U.S., 1870 to 1891. Urbana, Ill., 1937.
Deals chiefly with works brought out in various series or "libraries" which were counterparts of the contemporary paperback series of reprints.

14.8   Schick, Frank L.   The paperbound book in America and its European antecedents.   N.Y., 1958.

14.9   Sheehan, Donald.   This was publishing: a chronicle of the book trade in the Gilded Age.   Bloomington, Ind., 1952.

From the Civil War to World War I; largely material on four firms: Holt, Harper, Scribner, Dodd, Mead.   (There are, of course, many individual histories of various publishing companies.)

14.10   Cheney, O. H.   Economic survey of the book industry 1930-1931.   N.Y., 1931; [1961].

Reprinted also in 1949 with a statistical report for 1947-1948.   The 1961 reprint contains new appendixes and an index providing opportunities for "then and now" comparisons.

14.11   Miller, William.   The book industry.   N.Y., 1949.

Commercial and editorial aspects of publishing, including relations with public libraries and book clubs.

14.12   Grannis, Chandler B., ed.   What happens in book publishing.   N.Y., 1957.

A group of specialists explain operations in the American book-publishing business, from securing of manuscripts and copy editing to university press, book clubs, paperback markets, and distribution of U.S. books abroad.   Each chapter has a bibliography appended.

14.13   "Trends in American book publishing."   Library trends, v. 7, no. 1 (July, 1958).

A series of essays by various authorities on recent developments in the several areas of publishing.   Each essay is followed by a list of references. Frank L. Schick served as general editor of the issue.

14.14   American book-prices current.   N.Y., 1895———.

Annual record of books, MSS, etc. sold at auction in N.Y., Boston, and Philadelphia, with records of prices paid.   Various indexes of its contents have been published.

14.15   McKay, George L.   American book auction catalogues 1713-1934: a union list.   N.Y., 1937.

Supplements have appeared in the N.Y. Public Library *Bulletin,* v. 50 (1946) and v. 52 (1948).   (The library of the American Antiquarian Society, Worcester, Mass., contains one of the largest collections of American book dealers' catalogs.)

14.16   Private book collectors in the U.S. and Canada.   10th rev. ed.   N.Y., 1953.

One section arranges the collectors by their specialties—such as Southwestern Americana, drama, Mark Twain, Henry James.   The list is incomplete.

14.17   Mott, Frank L.   Golden multitudes: the story of best sellers in the U.S.   N.Y., 1947; [1960].

A standard study.

14.18   Hart, James D.   The popular book: a history of America's literary taste. N.Y., 1950; Berkeley, Calif., 1961.

Relates popular taste in reading to the "social pressures."

14.19   Hackett, Alice P.   60 years of best sellers, 1895-1955. N.Y., 1956.

Primarily lists of books; must be used with caution, for authentic figures on sales are often not available.

14.20   Kerr, Chester.   A report on American university presses. [Washington], 1949.

Based on a survey conducted in 1948-1949. Brought nearer to date in a pamphlet by the same author, *American University Publishing 1955*, [Ann Arbor, Mich., 1956].

14.21   Welter, Rush.   Problems of scholarly publication in the humanities and the social sciences. N.Y., [1959].

A factual report prepared for a committee of the American Council of Learned Societies; deals with periodicals as well as books.

See also 30.5, 32.5, 32.35.

15. SELECTED HISTORIES OF IDEAS IN THE U.S.

15.1   Curti, Merle.   The growth of American thought.   2d ed.   N.Y., [1951].

A standard work on the history of ideas in the U.S.   Special attention should be directed to its bibliography, which is both chronological and topical.   Arthur Bestor discusses intellectual history to 1900 (pp. 133-156) and Ralph H. Gabriel ideas and culture in the 20th century (pp. 312-328) in essays included in *Interpreting and Teaching American History: 31st Yearbook of the National Council for the Social Studies,* ed. William H. Cartwright and Richard L. Watson, Jr., Washington, [1961].   Selective bibliography.

15.2   Gabriel, Ralph H.   The course of American democratic thought.   2d ed.   N.Y., [1956].

Literature is included, along with other factors in social history.

15.3   Horton, Rod W., and Edwards, Herbert W.   Backgrounds of American literary thought.   N.Y., [1952].

Elementary historical treatments of Puritanism, the Enlightenment, Transcendentalism, Evolution and Pragmatism, Gentility and Revolt, Imperialism, Naturalism, and Freudianism.

15.4   Parrington, Vernon L.   Main currents in American thought.   3 v. [N.Y., 1927-1930; 1954]; v. 3 only [1963].

Survey of the political and social philosophy of American authors from Colonial times to about 1880.   Last volume unfinished.   (This work is often mistaken for a history of literature.)

15.5   Commager, Henry S.   The American mind: an interpretation of American thought and character since the 1880's.   New Haven, Conn., [1950; 1959].

Selected aspects of American thought are discussed, and a considerable portion is devoted to literature.   To a certain degree this continues Parrington to the 1940's.

15.6   Wish, Harvey.   Society and thought in America.   2 v.   N.Y., 1950-1952; v. 2 revised, N.Y., 1962.

An intellectual history which stresses the social conditioning of American ideas.

15.7   Lerner, Max. America as a civilization: life and thought in the U.S. today. N.Y., 1957; 2 v., 1960.

An attempt to grasp "the pattern and inner meaning of contemporary American civilization and its relation to the world of today." The bibliography adds many recent works to the record.

15.8   Persons, Stow. American minds: a history of ideas. N.Y., [1958].

An introduction to the history of American thought which describes "the principal focal concentrations of ideas," from the "colonial religious mind, 1620-1660" to the "contemporary neodemocratic mind." Very selective.

15.9   Beard, Charles A., and Beard, Mary R. The American spirit: a study of the idea of civilization in the U.S. N.Y., 1942; [1962].

This is v. 4 of a work entitled *The Rise of American Civilization.*

15.10   Dorfman, Joseph. The economic mind in American civilization. 5 v. N.Y., 1946-1959.

History of economic ideas, popular and technical, from 1606 to 1933.

15.11   Hofstadter, Richard. Social Darwinism in American thought. Rev. ed. N.Y., 1955; 1959.

15.12   Persons, Stow, ed. Evolutionary thought in America. New Haven, Conn., 1950; N.Y., 1956.

A symposium and bibliography.

15.13   Egbert, Donald D., and Persons, Stow, eds. Socialism and American life. 2 v. Princeton, N.J., 1952.

V. 1 is a symposium, including also outlines of European backgrounds; v. 2 is an uneven bibliography.

15.14   Hofstadter, Richard. The American political tradition and the men who made it. N.Y., 1948; 1958.

15.15   Hartz, Louis. The liberal tradition in America: an interpretation of American political thought since the Revolution. N.Y., [1955].

A suggestive hypothesis is outlined.

15.16   Rossiter, Clinton L. Conservatism in America. 2d ed. rev. N.Y., 1962.

Includes a discussion of the contemporary "New Conservatism."

15.17   Padover, Saul K. The genius of America: men whose ideas shaped our civilization, N. Y., [1960].

Among the men are Emerson, Thoreau, and Whitman.

15.18   Lewis, Richard W. B. The American Adam: innocence, tragedy and tradition in the nineteenth century. [Chicago, 1955; 1959].

"Tentative outlines of a native American mythology" as exhibited chiefly in certain aspects of literature. Rich with suggestions.

15.19   Lynn, Kenneth S. The dream of success: a study of the modern American imagination. Boston, [1955].

Dreiser, London, Phillips, Norris, and Herrick as affected by the "success myth." There is a chapter on Horatio Alger. Occasionally suggestive.

15.20   Jones, Howard M. Ideas in America. Cambridge, Mass., 1944.

Fugitive essays collected under three headings: "The Need for Literary History," "Studies in the History of Ideas in America," and "The Responsibilities of Contemporary American Literature."

15.21   Bode, Carl. The anatomy of American popular culture, 1840-1861. Berkeley, Calif., 1959.

Surveys popular taste of the period and attempts to relate it with psychological factors.

15.22   White, Morton G. Social thought in America: the revolt against formalism. N.Y., 1949; [1957].

An effort to trace "the development of the leading ideas" of Charles A. Beard, John Dewey, O. W. Holmes, Jr., James H. Robinson, and Thorstein Veblen.

15.23   May, Henry F. The end of American innocence: a study of the first years of our own time, 1912-1917. N.Y., 1959.

Illustrates the thesis that a wholesale repudiation of past values started in this period.

15.24   Haney, Robert W. Comstockery in America: patterns of censorship and control. Boston, [1960].

Sketchy, but contains a useful bibliography. Cf. also James C. N. Paul and Murray L. Schwartz, *Federal Censorship: Obscenity in the Mail*, N.Y., 1961.

16. PHILOSOPHY AND PSYCHOLOGY IN THE U.S.

16.1   Schneider, Herbert W.   A history of American philosophy.   2d ed. N.Y., 1963.

16.2   Anderson, Paul R., and Fisch, Max H., eds.   Philosophy in America from the Puritans to James, with representative selections.   N.Y., [1939].
Has useful bibliographies.

16.3   Townsend, Harvey G.   Philosophical ideas in the U.S.   N.Y., [1934].
Better on more recent movements than on earlier: account slightly Hegelian.

16.4   Werkmeister, William H.   A history of philosophical ideas in America. N.Y., [1949].
Fullest account of the period 1867-1939.   Chapters 17 and 18, on Neo-Realism and Critical Realism, are the most valuable portions.

16.5   Riley, I. Woodbridge.   American thought from Puritanism to Pragmatism and beyond.   2d ed.   N.Y., 1923; Gloucester, Mass., 1959.

16.6   Van Wesep, Henry B.   Seven sages: the story of American philosophy: Franklin, Emerson, James, Dewey, Santayana, Peirce, and Whitehead. N.Y., 1960.
A popular treatment, occasionally suggestive.

16.7   Fisch, Max H., ed.   Classic American philosophers.   N.Y., [1951].
Scholarly anthology representing Peirce, James, Royce, Santayana, Dewey, and Whitehead.

16.8   Moore, Edward C.   American pragmatism: Peirce, James, and Dewey. N.Y., 1961.
A study of underlying doctrines.

16.9   Perry, Ralph B.   The thought and character of William James.   2 v. Boston, 1935; [1962].
Provides the best means of getting the background for American philosophy in its most creative period.   Reprinted in briefer form, Cambridge, Mass., 1948.

16.10   Riley, I. Woodbridge.   American philosophy: the early schools.   N.Y., 1907; 1958.
Out of date but contains material not available elsewhere.

16.11   Curti, Merle. "The great Mr. Locke: America's philosopher, 1783-1861." Huntington Library bulletin, no. 11, pp. 107-157 (April, 1937).

16.12   Adams, George P., and Montague, William P., eds. Contemporary American philosophy: personal statements. 2 v. London and N.Y., [1930]; N.Y., [1961].
Statements of belief by 34 philosophers.

16.13   Kallen, Horace M., and Hook, Sidney, eds. American philosophy today and tomorrow. N.Y., [1935].
Statements of belief by 25 thinkers.

16.14   Fadiman, Clifton, ed. I believe: the personal philosophies of certain eminent men and women of our time. N.Y., 1939.
Contains statements of belief by Pearl Buck, Ellen Glasgow, Santayana, and James Thurber and revised statements by Dreiser, Mencken, and other Americans, Europeans, and Asians.

16.15   Hook, Sidney, ed. American philosophers at work: the philosophic scene in the U.S. N.Y., [1956].

16.16   Roback, Abraham A. History of American psychology. N.Y., [1952].
Uneven and sometimes biased. (Brief autobiographies, mentioning influences, etc. of selected prominent psychologists of Europe and the U.S. appear in *A History of Psychology in Autobiography,* ed. Carl A. Murchison, 3 v., Worcester, Mass., 1930-1936; N.Y., 1961.)

16.17   Boring, Edwin G. A history of experimental psychology. 2d ed. N.Y., [1950].
A standard work containing special chapters on the establishment of "modern psychology" in America.

16.18   Wells, Harry K. Psychoanalysis in the U.S. N.Y., 1962.
Primarily concerned with Karen Horney, Erich Fromm, and Harry S. Sullivan.

16.19   Oberndorf, Clarence P. A history of psychoanalysis in America. N.Y., 1953.
Written by a clinician whose personal experiences enter into his record of events.

16.20   Fay, Jay W. American psychology before William James. New Brunswick, N. J., 1939.

16.21   Davies, John D. Phrenology: fad and science: a 19th-century American crusade. New Haven, Conn., 1955.
(Poe, Whitman, and other writers of their day were greatly influenced by phrenology.)

17. TRANSCENDENTALISM IN THE U.S.

17.1 Hutchison, William R. The transcendentalist ministers: church reform in the New England renaissance. New Haven, Conn., 1959.

A well-rounded account of Transcendentalism in its chief manifestation. The bibliography is the most adequate one on the subject.

17.2 Cooke, George W. Unitarianism in America: a history of its origin and development. Boston, 1902.

An excellent account of 19th-century developments, with a special chapter on "Unitarianism and Literature." Provides a neat history of the emergence of Transcendentalism.

17.3 Wilbur, Earl M. A history of Unitarianism in Transylvania, England, and America. Cambridge, Mass., 1952.

17.4 Frothingham, Octavius B. Transcendentalism in New England: a history. N.Y., 1876; 1959.

17.5 Goddard, Harold C. Studies in New England transcendentalism. N.Y., 1908; 1960.

17.6 Ellis, Charles M. An essay on transcendentalism (1842). Ed. Walter Harding. Gainesville, Fla., 1954.

A reprint of one of the better treatments emanating from the 1840's.

17.7 Miller, Perry, ed. The American transcendentalists, their prose and poetry. Cambridge, Mass., 1950; Garden City, N.Y., 1957.

An anthology with a suggestive introduction. The first edition bears the title *The Transcendentalists: An Anthology.*

17.8 Leighton, Walter L. French philosophers and New-England transcendentalism. Charlottesville, Va., 1908.

Deals with the very important influence of Victor Cousin and other Frenchmen.

17.9 Wells, Ronald V. Three Christian transcendentalists: James Marsh, Caleb Sprague Henry, Frederic Henry Hedge. N.Y., 1943.

17.10 Persons, Stow. Free religion, an American faith. New Haven, Conn., 1947; Boston [1963].

(Free religion eventually absorbed many of the later Transcendentalists.)

See also 12.13, 15.3, 21.15, 29.1, 32.30, 32.33, 32.72.

18. RELIGION IN THE U.S.

18.1   Burr, Nelson R. A critical bibliography of religion in America. 2 v. Princeton, N.J., 1961.

The most extensive bibliography of the subject, with profuse comment, at times excessive in both quantity and the charity bestowed upon the books and articles discussed. The first volume surveys guides, general histories, etc. and then turns to individual denominations and sects. The second volume treats religion in American life and culture, including the arts, literature, and intellectual history. This bibliography forms part of the following item.

18.2   Smith, James W., and Jameson, A. Leland, eds. Religion in American life. 4 v. Princeton, N.J., 1961.

A loosely organized and uneven symposium of papers centered on two topics: "The Shaping of American Religion" and "Religious Perspectives in American Culture." Under the latter category, e.g., appear exploratory or tentative discussions of religious poetry, the Bible in fiction, and religious novels as best sellers.

18.3   Olmstead, Clifton E. History of religion in the U.S. Englewood Cliffs, N.J., 1960.

A general, textbook survey, with a sociological slant and an up-to-date selective bibliography.

18.4   Gaustad, Edwin S. Historical atlas of religion in America. N.Y., [1962].

Invaluable for its pictorial representation of the distribution of the sects at various times in the past; equipped with bibliographical and statistical information.

18.5   Smith, H. Shelton, *et al.*, eds. American Christianity. 2 v. N.Y., 1960-1963.

An anthology of representative documents, both Catholic and Protestant, with historical introductions and extensive bibliographies classified according to various periods and movements.

18.6   Hudson, Winthrop S. American Protestantism. Chicago, [1961].
A compact survey notable for its readability.

18.7   Morais, Herbert M. Deism in eighteenth century America. N.Y., 1934.

18.8   Koch, G. Adolf.   Republican religion: the American Revolution and the cult of reason. N.Y., [1933].

Deism and the reaction against it.

18.9   Billington, Ray A.   The Protestant crusade, 1800-1860: a study of the origins of American nativism.   N.Y., 1938; Gloucester, Mass., 1963.

Treats the opposition to Catholicism which was part of the Know-Nothing movement.

18.10   Post, Albert.   Popular freethought in America 1825-1850.   N.Y., 1943.

18.11   Warren, Sidney.   American freethought, 1860-1914.   N.Y., 1943.

18.12   Hopkins, Charles H.   The rise of the social gospel in American Protestantism 1865-1915.   New Haven, Conn., 1940.

Deals with the "progressive" theology and sociological tendencies resulting from the impact of industrial society and scientific theories.

18.13   Garrison, Winfred E.   The march of faith: the story of religion in America since 1865.   N.Y., 1933.

Represents a species of social history emphasizing changes within denominational lines.

18.14   Schneider, Herbert W.   Religion in 20th century America.   Cambridge, Mass., 1952.

A volume in the Library of Congress series in American Civilization; useful for suggestions.

18.15   Ellis, John T.   A guide to American Catholic history.   Milwaukee, 1959.

The same compiler has prepared *Documents of American Catholic History,* Milwaukee, [1956].

18.16   Mead, Frank S.   Handbook of denominations in the U.S.   2d rev. ed. N.Y., [1961].

Brief sketches of 200-odd sects or denominations.   (Annual statistics appear in *Yearbook of the Churches,* published by the National Council of the Churches of Christ in the U.S.A.)

18.17   Mayer, Frederick E.   The religious bodies of America.   St. Louis, [1954].

Various denominations are treated from the angle of their theology; bibliographies are appended to each section; intended "primarily for the theological student and the parish minister."

18.18   Stewart, Randall. American literature & Christian doctrine.   Baton Rouge, La., [1958].

A tentative exploration of several authors and literary traditions in terms of their religious ideas. American literature is in part considered also by Amos N. Wilder in *The Spiritual Aspects of the New Poetry,* N.Y., [1940]; *Modern Poetry and the Christian Tradition,* N.Y., 1952; and *Theology and Modern Literature,* Cambridge, Mass., 1958.

18.19   Strong, Augustus H. American poets and their theology. Philadelphia, 1916.

Treats, in an old-fashioned way, Bryant, Emerson, Whittier, Poe, Longfellow, Lowell, Holmes, Lanier, and Whitman.

18.20   Luccock, Halford E. Contemporary American literature and religion. Chicago, 1934.

Occasionally suggestive.

18.21   Luccock, Halford E. American mirror: social, ethical and religious aspects of American literature, 1930-1940. N.Y., 1940.

A sequel to the preceding item.

See also 17.10.

19. ARTS OTHER THAN LITERATURE

19.1 The art index: a cumulative author and subject index to a selected list of fine arts periodicals and museum bulletins 1929/1930——. N.Y., 1930——.
Standard bibliography for the several fine arts.

19.2 Chamberlin, Mary W. Guide to art reference books. Chicago, 1959. Includes a section on the U.S.

19.3 Larkin, Oliver W. Art and life in America. Rev. ed. N.Y., [1960].
Introductory survey of the history of architecture, sculpture, painting, and, sporadically, the minor arts; intended for the use of students of American Civilization. Bibliographies and illustrations add value. (The Archives of American Art, housed in the Detroit Institute of Arts, is collecting in one central place records of American painters, sculptors, and craftsmen, such as original and microfilm source materials, biographies, catalogs, and photographs of works of art.)

19.4 Mendelowitz, Daniel M. A history of American art. N.Y., [1960].
A clearly written but sketchy history of the visual arts which contains bibliographical references for each of its sections.

19.5 Pierson, William H., and Davidson, Martha, eds. Arts of the U.S.: a pictorial survey. N.Y., [1960].
Eighteen historical essays by a variety of experts are followed by a huge display of illustrative pictures—all of them separately available in color on slides. Stage design, photography, and costume design are included.

19.6 Mumford, Lewis. The brown decades: a study of the arts in America, 1865-1895. 2d rev. ed. N.Y., [1955]; Gloucester, Mass., [1960].
Useful largely as an over-all interpretation of the period.

19.7 Gilbert, Dorothy B., ed. Who's who in American art. 8th ed. N.Y., 1962.
Sculptors, painters, graphic artists, writers and historians of art, museum personnel, cartoonists, illustrators of books, educators are included but not architects, photographers, and decorators. A regional index also appears, arranged alphabetically by state and city. New editions now appear triennially. (For architects see 19.36.)

19.8   Groce, George C., and Wallace, David H.   The New-York Historical Society's dictionary of artists in America, 1564-1860.   New Haven, Conn., 1957.

Biographical dictionary of painters, sculptors, engravers, etc., amateur and professional, to 1860.

19.9   Christensen, Erwin O.   The index of American design.   Washington, 1950; N.Y., 1950; 1959.

Describes and reproduces numerous examples of the holdings of the Index of American Design, which is a collection of WPA drawings and paintings of a vast variety of products of crafts and folk art, now housed in the National Gallery of Art in Washington.

Painting and Drawing

19.10   Barker, Virgil.   American painting: history and interpretation.   N.Y., 1950; 1960.

Ends about 1900 with the work of Homer, Ryder, and Eakins.   (The Frick Art Reference Library, in New York, is the leading research library in its field.)

19.11   Richardson, Edgar P.   Painting in America: the story of 450 years.   N.Y., [1956].

The appended selective bibliography makes a special point of museum exhibition catalogs, which often contain reproductions of pictures.

19.12   Monro, Isabel S., and Monro, Kate M.   Index to reproductions of American paintings: a guide to pictures occurring in more than eight hundred books.   N.Y., 1948.

Occasionally locates the paintings in the permanent collections which house them.   Cf. 19.5.

19.13   Dunlap, William.   A history of the rise and progress of the arts of design in the U.S.   New ed.   3 v.   Boston, 1918.

Originally published in 1834, this is still valuable because of its firsthand accounts of artists of the late 18th and early 19th centuries.

19.14   Goodrich, Lloyd, and Baur, John I. H.   American art of our century.   N.Y., [1961].

19.15   Brown, Milton W.   American painting from the Armory Show to the Depression.   Princeton, N.J., 1955.

A history, chiefly of the realists, from the Ash Can School to the new realism, illustrated by T. H. Benton.

19.16   Janis, Sidney.   Abstract & surrealist art in America.   N.Y., [1944].

19.17   Weitenkampf, Frank.   American graphic art.   New ed.   N.Y., 1924.   Engraving and book illustration.

19.18   Murrell, William. A history of American graphic humor. 2 v. N.Y., 1933-1938.

Covers the chief cartoonists 1747-1938. See also Stephen D. Becker, *Comic Art in America: A Social History of the Funnies, the Political Cartoons, Magazine Humor, Sporting Cartoons, and Animated Cartoons,* N.Y., 1959, a popular survey.

19.19   Nevins, Allan, and Weitenkampf, Frank. A century of political cartoons: caricature in the U.S. from 1800 to 1900. N.Y., 1944.

An annotated list appears in Frank Weitenkampf, *Political Caricature in the U.S.,* N.Y., 1953, which originally appeared in the *Bulletin of the New York Public Library,* v. 56 (March-December, 1952).

Sculpture

19.20   McCausland, Elizabeth. "A selected bibliography on American painting and sculpture from Colonial times to the present." Magazine of art, v. 4, pp. 329-349 (November, 1946).

An uncritical check list; reprinted in *Who's Who in American Art,* Washington, 1947, v. 4, pp. 611-653.

19.21   Proske, Beatrice G. Brookgreen Gardens sculpture. Brookgreen, S.C., 1943, v. 2. Brookgreen, S.C., 1955.

Contains brief sketches and bibliographies of many sculptors 1870-1940. The second volume is a kind of supplement.

19.22   Taft, Lorado. The history of American sculpture. New ed. N.Y., 1930.

Taft was a sculptor—not a historian.

19.23   Gardner, Albert T. E. Yankee stonecutters: the first American school of sculpture, 1800-1850. N.Y., 1945.

The biographical sketches and the bibliography are also useful. Lists the early 19th-century American sculpture in the collection of the Metropolitan Museum.

19.24   Schnier, Jacques P. Sculpture in modern America. Berkeley, Calif., 1948.

Architecture

19.25   Burchard, John, and Bush-Brown, Albert. The architecture of America: a social and cultural history. Boston, [1961].

A popular treatise which often provides the background for, rather than, a history. Includes bibliography. Wayne Andrews, *Architecture in America,* N.Y., 1960, is a pictorial history from Colonial days to the present.

19.26   Hitchcock, Henry-Russell. American architectural books: a list of books, portfolios, and pamphlets on architecture and related subjects published in America before 1895. 3d rev. ed. Minneapolis, [1946]; [1962].

19.27   Roos, Frank J. Writings on early American architecture: an annotated list of books and articles on architecture constructed before 1860 in the eastern half of the U.S. Columbus, Ohio, 1943.

19.28   Tallmadge, Thomas E.   The story of architecture in America.   Rev. ed.   N.Y., [1936].

19.29   Giedion, Sigfried.   Space, time, and architecture: the growth of a new tradition.   4th ed. enlarged.   Cambridge, Mass., 1962.

Covers the western world from the 17th century to date, but the sections on the U.S. in the 19th and 20th centuries are valuable; discusses also city planning.

19.30   Morrison, Hugh.   Early American architecture: from the first Colonial settlements to the national period.   N.Y., 1952.

Standard work, covering the eastern colonies to the time of the Revolutionary War, French Louisiana to 1803, and the Spanish colonies to 1848.

19.31   Hamlin, Talbot F.   Greek revival architecture in America.   London and N.Y., 1944.

For the earlier 19th century.

19.32   Upjohn, Everard M.   Richard Upjohn, architect and churchman.   N.Y., 1939.

Contains considerable background material.

19.33   Hitchcock, Henry-Russell.   The architecture of H. H. Richardson and his times.   N.Y., 1936; Hamden, Conn., 1961.

19.34   Scully, Vincent J.   The shingle style: architectural theory and design from Richardson to the origins of Wright.   New Haven, Conn., 1955.

19.35   Fitch, James M.   American building: the forces that shape it.   Boston, 1948.

Gives emphasis to recent technological improvements.

19.36   Koyl, George S., ed.   American architects directory.   2d ed.   N.Y., 1962.

Appendixes list various schools of architecture and selected current journals in the field.

19.37   Mumford, Lewis, ed.   Roots of contemporary American architecture.   N.Y., [1952].

Thirty-seven essays by 29 writers, from mid-nineteenth century to 1950, having to do with the theory and philosophy of architecture.

19.38   Wright, Frank L.   Writings and buildings.   Selected by Edgar Kaufman and Ben Raeburn.   [N.Y., 1960].

A convenient summary of writings by or about the great innovator (1869-1959).   More than 150 illustrations.

19.39   Von Eckardt, Wolf, ed.   Mid-century architecture in America: honor awards of the American Institute of Architects, 1949-1961.   Baltimore, [1961].

Photographs, occasionally designs also, with brief sketches of the architects or firms to whom the awards have been given.

Music

19.40 Howard, John T. Our American music: three hundred years of it. 4th ed. rev. N.Y., [1955].

This is the most adequate general history of the subject; it may be generally supplemented by Chase.

19.41 Chase, Gilbert. America's music from the Pilgrims to the present. N.Y., [1955].

Supplements Howard from time to time, and its approach is different.

19.42 Mueller, John H. The American symphony orchestra: a social history of musical taste. Bloomington, Ind., 1951.

19.43 Hipsher, Edward E. American opera and its composers. Philadelphia, [1934].

Surveys the history of serious opera and offers a "summary of the lighter forms which led up to its birth."

19.44 Mates, Julian. The American musical stage before 1800. New Brunswick, N.J., [1962].

Not a history of opera.

19.45 Green, Stanley. The world of musical comedy: the story of the American musical stage as told through the careers of its foremost composers and lyricists. N.Y., [1960].

See also 23.36.

19.46 Levine, Richard, and Simon, Alfred. Encyclopedia of theatre music: a comprehensive listing of more than 4000 songs from Broadway and Hollywood: 1900-1960. N.Y., [1961].

See also John Chipman, *Index to Top-Hit Tunes (1900-1950)*, Boston, [1962].

19.47 Mattfeld, Julius. Variety music calvacade, 1620-1961: a chronology of vocal and instrumental music popular in the U.S. Rev. ed. Englewood Cliffs, N.J., [1962].

19.48 Wilgus, Donald K. Anglo-American folksong scholarship since 1898. New Brunswick, N.J., 1959.

A survey of scholarship devoted to ballads and folksongs in English: theory, collectors, editors, etc. Eminent collections are described, and appendixes offer a discography of l. p. records, a bibliography, and a glossary of technical terms.

19.49 Lawless, Ray M. Folksingers and folksongs in America. N.Y., [1960].

Brief biographies of over 200 singers, a short account of folk-music instruments, a richly annotated bibliography, a listing of l. p. records, and a selected roster of song titles make this an almost ideal handbook for the serious-minded student without professional knowledge. Chapter 17 describes folklore societies and their journals as well as various folk festivals of the U.S.

19.50 Stearns, Marshall W. The story of jazz. N.Y., 1956.

Includes bibliographical references. Biographies of directors and performers appear in Leonard Feather, *The Encyclopedia of Jazz*, rev. ed., N.Y., 1960.

The acceptance of the "new art form" between the two World Wars especially is considered by Neil Leonard in *Jazz and the White Americans,* Chicago, [1962]. The evolution of the phonograph is surveyed in *From Tin Foil to Stereo,* by Oliver Read and Walter L. Welch, Indianapolis, [1959]. (Housed at Tulane University is an Archive of New Orleans Jazz.)

19.51 Edmunds, John, and Boelzner, Gordon. Some twentieth-century American composers: a selective bibliography. 2 v. N.Y., 1959-1960.

Consists chiefly of writings by or about selected composers.

19.52 American Society of Composers, Authors and Publishers. The ASCAP biographical dictionary of composers, authors, and publishers. Ed. Daniel I. McNamara. 2d ed. N.Y., [1952].

19.53 Reis, Claire. Composers in America: biographical sketches of contemporary composers with a record of their works. Rev. ed. N.Y., 1947.

19.54 Smith, Cecil M. Worlds of music. Philadelphia, [1952].

Music as a business: concert management, touring performers, etc.

19.55 Barzun, Jacques. Music in American life. Rev. ed. Bloomington, Ind., [1962].

A popular treatise dealing with the present day, not the past.

See also 8.1.

20. CHIEF GENERAL BIBLIOGRAPHIES OF AMERICAN LITERATURE

20.1 Johnson, Thomas H., ed. Literary history of the U.S. V. 3. N.Y., 1948; 1953; 1962.

The third volume of a standard history, this is exclusively devoted to bibliography. It is the most extensive bibliography of its subject and has a special section treating separately a considerable number of individual authors. Very well arranged but insufficiently indexed. The following item is a supplement. The 1962 issue is bound in with the supplement but separately paged.

20.2 Ludwig, Richard M., ed. Literary history of the U.S.: bibliography supplement. N.Y., 1959; 1962.

A supplement to v. 3 of *LHUS* which assembles new material published since 1948 and adds comprehensive bibliographies of 16 new authors.

20.3 Quinn, Arthur H., ed. The literature of the American people: an historical and critical survey. N.Y., [1951].

Contains a 120-page bibliography with critical comments, prepared by the four authors of the volume.

20.4 The Cambridge history of American literature. Ed. William P. Trent *et al.* 4 v. N.Y., 1917-1921.

Bibliographies, arranged by chapters, appear at end of v. 1, 2, and 4. Both text and bibliographies are often, but not always, outmoded, especially as they concern major figures. In 1944 the three volumes were reprinted in one, without the bibliographies.

20.5 Leary, Lewis G. Articles on American literature 1900-1950. Durham, N.C., 1954.

Conflates lists from *PMLA, American Literature,* and other sources. (For articles since 1950, see *PMLA* annual bibliography and the quarterly check lists in *American Literature.*) A revised edition covering 1900-1963 is due from the Duke University Press in 1964.

20.6 American literature. 1929———.

The chief journal in its field, published quarterly by the Duke University Press, with the co-operation of the American Literature Group of the Modern Language Association of America. Contains articles of an historical, critical, or bibliographical sort, book reviews, lists of dissertations completed or in progress and an annotated check list of current periodical articles. (To 1951 the articles listed in its bibliography have been conflated in Leary.) The first 22 v. of the journal have been reprinted by the Kraus Reprint Corporation, New York City, and v. 23 through 29 will shortly be available also.

20.7 Marshall, Thomas F. An analytical index to American Literature, v. 1-30 (March, 1929—January, 1959). Durham, N.C., 1963.

Indexes by author and subject the articles published in the journal and the chief books reviewed in it.

20.8 "American bibliography for 1921———." PMLA, v. 37———, 1922———.

Annual listing of books and articles on various modern European languages and literatures; until 1957 largely limited to works by Americans. Carries regularly a special section on American literature.

20.9 Woodress, James. Dissertations in American literature 1891-1955 with supplement 1956-1961. Durham, N.C., 1962.

A classified list of doctoral dissertations from about 100 universities at home and abroad, including an incomplete listing of those in progress prior to 1956. (For more recent dissertations, see the lists published quarterly in *American Literature.*)

20.10 American writers series. General editor, Harry H. Clark. N.Y., etc., [1934-1950]; N.Y., 1961———.

A series of textbooks, most of which are devoted to individual authors, from Edwards and Franklin to Harte and James; selected writings plus carefully prepared introductions and annotated selective bibliographies. Various scholars edited the several volumes. To the date of their publication the bibliographies are exceptionally well chosen from the supply of both books and articles. The reprints currently appearing are part of the American Century Series of Hill and Wang, Publishers, and some of them have substantially revised bibliographies.

20.11 Blanck, Jacob. Bibliography of American literature. 8 or 9 v. planned. New Haven, Conn., 1955———.

Descriptive bibliographies of all first editions and various other separates of about 300 authors of belles-lettres who died before 1931. A most accurate work, with invaluable lists. Locates copies in selected libraries. The first volume covers 41 authors, Henry Adams to Donn Byrne; the second (1957), 45 authors, G. W. Cable to Timothy Dwight; the third (1959), 34 authors, Eggleston to Bret Harte; the fourth (1963), 18, Hawthorne to Ingraham.

20.12 Johnson, Merle D. American first editions. 4th ed. Rev. and enlarged by Jacob Blanck. N.Y., 1942; Cambridge, Mass., 1962.

Lists the chief first editions of 194 American authors of the 19th and 20th centuries. The 1936 edition contained 24 authors omitted from this one, including Ray S. Baker, Zona Gale, Mary N. Murfree, D. G. Phillips, Upton Sinclair. Will eventually be wholly displaced by Blanck.

20.13 Foley, Patrick K. American authors 1795-1895: a bibliography of first and notable editions chronologically arranged with notes. Boston, 1897.

Still useful for works by certain minor authors.

20.14 Jones, Joseph, *et al.* American literary manuscripts: a checklist of holdings in academic, historical and public libraries in the U.S. Austin, Texas, [1960].

A calendar of the holdings of various libraries, prepared by a committee of the American Literature Group of the MLA presently headed by J. Albert Robbins, Indiana University, which plans a supplement. See also Hamer, *A Guide to Archives and Manuscripts in the U.S.* (1.14), *National Union Catalog of Manuscript Collections* (1.13), Carman and Thompson, *A Guide to the Principal Sources for American Civilization, 1800-1900, in the City of New York: Manuscripts* (8.3), and Crick and Alman, *A Guide to Manuscripts Relating to America in Great Britain and Ireland* (8.4). (George Hendrick, University of Frankfurt, is compiling a list of American literary MSS in Continental libraries).

20.15 Northup, Clark S. A register of bibliographies of the English language and literature. New Haven, Conn., 1925; N.Y., 1962.

Includes various American authors and topics, such as Negro literature, printing and publishing, local literature.

20.16 Van Patten, Nathan. An index to bibliographies and bibliographical contributions relating to the work of American and British authors, 1923-1932. Stanford, Calif., 1934.

Works included were printed 1923-1932, plus a very few from 1933.

20.17 Stovall, Floyd, ed. Eight American authors, a review of research and criticism. N.Y., 1956; 1963.

An excellent bibliographical survey of studies on Poe, Emerson, Hawthorne, Thoreau, Melville, Whitman, Mark Twain, and Henry James. Each of the 8 authors is treated by a distinguished scholar. The reprint contains a bibliographical supplement compiled by J. Chesley Matthews—a selective check list, 1955-1962.

20.18 Spargo, John W. A bibliographical manual for students of the language and literature of England and the U.S.: a short-title list. 3d ed. N.Y., 1956.

Deals primarily with English literature and is out of date. Similar manuals are: Tom P. Cross, *Bibliographical Guide to English Studies,* 10th ed., Chicago, [1956]; and Arthur G. Kennedy and Donald B. Sands, *A Concise Bibliography for Students of English,* 4th ed., Stanford, Calif., [1960]. Briefer and more recent are Donald F. Bond, *A Reference Guide to English Studies,* Chicago, [1962], which supplants Cross; and Richard D. Altick and Andrew Wright, *Selective Bibliography for the Study of English and American Literature,* 2d ed., N.Y., [1963], briefest one of the sort and equipped with a short glossary of "useful terms."

20.19 Contemporary literary scholarship: a critical review. Ed. Lewis G. Leary for a committee of the National Council of Teachers of English. N.Y., [1958].

Brief surveys, by various hands, of recent publications in the fields of English, comparative, and American literature. The material on Americana, a minority element in the book, must be used with caution, for there are many gaps in information and the critical appraisals are sometimes rather partisan.

21. CHIEF GENERAL HISTORIES AND SELECTED CRITICAL DISCUSSIONS OF AMERICAN LITERATURE

21.1 Crawford, Bartholow V., *et al.* American literature. 3d ed. N.Y., [1953]; [1957].

An outline of the history of American literature. Earlier editions bear the title *An Outline-History of American Literature.*

21.2 Literary history of the U.S. Ed. Robert E. Spiller, Willard Thorp, Thomas H. Johnson, *et al.* 3 v. N.Y., 1948.

Usually referred to as *LHUS.* Fifty-five authors contributed one or more chapters, which vary in quality but make up the most extensive academic history of the subject. The third volume is exclusively devoted to bibliography.

21.3 Literary history of the U.S. Ed. Robert E. Spiller *et al.* Rev. ed. in one v. N.Y., 1953.

A new chapter, "Postscript at Mid-century," and a 23-page bibliography for the general reader represent the chief changes. V. 3 of the 1948 edition is not included; cf. 20.1.

21.4 Quinn, Arthur H., ed. The literature of the American people: an historical and critical survey. N.Y., [1951].

Written by four scholars, Kenneth B. Murdock, Arthur H. Quinn, Clarence Gohdes, and George F. Whicher, this is in method the most scholarly narrative of the literature of the U.S.

21.5 Spiller, Robert E. The cycle of American literature. N.Y., 1955; 1957.

An excellent short history, along with a partial elaboration of a theory of cycles.

21.6 Taylor, Walter F. The story of American letters. Chicago, 1956.

Revised edition of an historical survey originally [1936] entitled *A History of American Letters.* Uses the Colonial period merely as a point of departure and ends with authors established at the time of World War II.

21.7 Howard, Leon. Literature and the American tradition. Garden City, N.Y., 1960; [1963].

A short comprehensive history which, in part, undertakes to "seek out those attitudes of mind which controlled the creative imagination and helped shape the country's literature toward a recognizable national character."

21.8   Lüdeke, Henry. Geschichte der amerikanischen Literatur. 2d ed. Bern, [1963].

The most consequential history of its subject ever written by a foreigner; especially valuable for its references to German backgrounds.

21.9   Arnavon, Cyrille. Histoire littéraire des États-Unis. [Paris, 1953]. Best general history of the subject written by a Frenchman.

21.10   Cunliffe, Marcus. The literature of the U.S. Rev. ed. London, etc., [1959].

A brief account, written by an Englishman, useful for occasional criticisms.

21.11   Brooks, Van Wyck. Makers and finders: a history of the writer in America, 1800-1915.

A series of 5 v. containing a well-written, impressionistic history in which many minor writers are interwoven. The scholar usually finds the treatment of the minor authors more rewarding factually than the discussion of the major figures. As a venture in criticism in the broader sense, the series is the most extensive as well as the most brilliantly written survey of its subject ever produced by a single author. The 5 v. in the order of coverage are: *The World of Washington Irving*, N.Y., [1944]; *The Flowering of New England, 1815-1865*, new and rev. ed., N.Y., 1937; *The Times of Melville and Whitman*, N.Y., 1947; *New England: Indian Summer, 1865-1915*, N.Y., 1940; *The Confident Years: 1885-1915*, N.Y., 1952. All of these have been reprinted, e.g., in Everyman's Library.

21.12   Pattee, Fred L. A history of American literature since 1870. N.Y., 1915.

Still very helpful, though it must be used in connection with the following item.

21.13   Pattee, Fred L. The new American literature, 1890-1930. N.Y., [1930].

A vigorous critical and historical account. In certain cases this reassesses authors and works published prior to 1890.

21.14   Foerster, Norman, ed. The reinterpretation of American literature. N.Y., 1928; 1959.

Contains essays on the influence of Puritanism, the frontier, etc. This work was very influential on the academic study of American literature for a number of years.

21.15   Clark, Harry H., ed. Transitions in American literary history. Durham, N.C., 1953.

A symposium of 7 exploratory essays, by various scholars, on "The Decline of Puritanism," "The Late Eighteenth Century," "The Decline of Neoclassicism," "The Rise of Romanticism," "The Rise of Transcendentalism," "The Decline of Romantic Idealism," and "The Rise of Realism 1871-1891."

21.16   Hart, James D. The Oxford companion to American literature. 3d ed. N.Y., 1956.

The standard handbook; includes sketches of authors and magazines, outlines of plots, explanations of movements and terminology.

21.17   Herzberg, Max J., *et al.*, eds. The reader's encyclopedia of American literature. N.Y., [1962].

An exceedingly uneven collection of entries, chiefly biographical, a few by capable authorities. Many of the authors listed have little or nothing to do with belles-lettres. Occasionally useful in supplementing Hart's *Oxford Companion.* See also 11.13.

21.18   Wilson, Edmund, ed. The shock of recognition: the development of literature in the U.S. recorded by the men who made it. 2 v. N.Y., [1955]; 1961.

A collection of literary documents by distinguished American authors commenting on other authors. V. 1 covers 1845-1900; v. 2 the 20th century.

21.19   Howells, William D. Literary friends and acquaintance: a personal retrospect of American authorship. N.Y., 1900; 1902.

Contains much first-hand material on Boston and New York as literary centers 1860-1900 and presents invaluable portraits of Holmes, Longfellow, and Lowell in old age.

21.20   Garland, Hamlin. Roadside meetings. N.Y., 1930; Companions on the trail. N.Y., 1931; My friendly contemporaries. N.Y., 1932; Afternoon neighbors. N.Y., 1934.

A series of recollections of authors and literary history covering "the purely literary side" of Garland's experiences during the period 1885-1930.

21.21   Knight, Grant C. The critical period in American literature. Chapel Hill, N.C., [1951].

Literary history of the decade 1890-1900. (For a sequel covering the following decade, see 28.10.)

21.22   Macy, John, ed. American writers on American literature. N.Y., [1931].

Thirty-seven writers contributed a chapter each, on an important author or topic like Colonial historians or contemporary poetry. One of the better ventures of the sort.

21.23   Matthiessen, Francis O. American renaissance. N.Y., [1941; 1957].

A standard critical study concerned with Emerson, Hawthorne, Melville, Thoreau, and Whitman.

21.24   Brownell, William C. American prose masters. N.Y., 1909; Cambridge, Mass., 1963.

Discriminating essays on Cooper, Hawthorne, Emerson, Poe, Lowell, and Henry James.

21.25   Miller, Perry. The raven and the whale: the war of words and wits in the era of Poe and Melville. N.Y., [1956]; [1962].

21.26   University of Minnesota pamphlets on American writers. Ed. William V. O'Connor *et al.* Minneapolis, 1959———.

A series of brief pamphlets each dealing with a single author and containing biography, "simple, easily got at critical introductions," and bibliography of the author's books and of articles and books about him. The pamphlets are prepared by various critics, chiefly college professors.

21.27   The American authors and critics series. Ed. Foster Provost and John Mahoney. N.Y., 1961——.

Each volume, of about 150 pages, is aimed to provide an "introduction and interpretation" and is equipped with selective bibliographical material. Various college teachers are the authors.

21.28   Twayne's United States authors series. Ed. Sylvia E. Bowman. N.Y., 1961——.

More than 200 volumes are planned, each of about 150 to 200 pages, largely critical and interpretative and equipped with notes and selective bibliography. The authors, chiefly younger college teachers, vary considerably in capacity. Steinbeck, Eudora Welty, Zona Gale, and Joseph Kirkland appear as subjects side by side with Franklin, Cooper, Poe, and Whitman. Works on general topics are also planned for later inclusion.

See also 8.1, 20.3-4, 20.6, and 20.10.

22. POETRY

22.1   Granger's index to poetry. 5th ed. N.Y., 1962.

Indexes contents of 574 anthologies of verse, through June 30, 1960, by title of poem and first line, author, and subject. Principally British and American poetry.

22.2   Stedman, Edmund C. Poets of America. Boston and N.Y., 1885.

Old but still useful, both as history and commentary, especially on Bryant, Whittier, Emerson, Longfellow, Poe, Holmes, Lowell, Whitman, and Bayard Taylor.

22.3   Kreymborg, Alfred. A history of American poetry: our singing strength. N.Y., 1934.

In 1929 this book appeared under the title *Our Singing Strength*. To be used with caution.

22.4   Pearce, Roy H. The continuity of American poetry. Princeton, N.J., 1961.

A purposefully unhistorical discussion of the tradition of American poetry in relation to the national culture. More valuable for certain parts than for the whole.

22.5   Allen, Gay W. American prosody. N.Y., [1935].

Versification of 11 poets, from Freneau to Emily Dickinson.

22.6   Wells, Henry W. The American way of poetry. N.Y., 1943.

Uneven survey of the "indigenous and unique," with good critical chapters on Freneau, Whitman, Emerson, Emily Dickinson, *et al.*

22.7   Kuntz, Joseph M. Poetry explication: a checklist of interpretations since 1925 of British and American poems past and present. Rev. ed. Denver, 1962.

(A periodical entitled the *Explicator*, 1942——, is especially devoted to "explication"; a considerable portion of the poems treated is American. The June issues contain an annual check list of "explication.")

22.8   Hastings, Henry C. Spoken poetry on records and tapes: an index of currently available recordings. Chicago, 1957.

22.9   Conner, Frederick W. Cosmic optimism: a study of the interpretation of evolution by American poets from Emerson to Robinson. Gainesville, Fla., 1949.

22.10   Lenhart, Charmenz S. Musical influence on American poetry. Athens, Ga., [1956].

22.11   Wegelin, Oscar. Early American poetry. 2d ed. rev. and enlarged. 2 v. N.Y., 1930; Gloucester, Mass., 1962.
Incomplete list of volumes of verse, 1650-1820.

22.12   Arms, George. The fields were green: a new view of Bryant, Whittier, Holmes, Lowell, and Longfellow, with a selection of their poems. Stanford, Calif., [1953].

22.13   Kindilien, Carlin T. American poetry in the eighteen nineties. Providence, R.I., 1956.
Based on the Harris Collection at Brown University, which is one of the largest special collections of poetry of the U.S.

Poetry, 20th Century

22.14   Irish, Wynot R. The modern American muse . . . 1900-1925. [Syracuse, N.Y., 1950].
Lists chronologically by year of publication 6,906 books of verse.

22.15   "American poetry: 1930-1940." Accent, v. 1, pp. 213-228 (Summer, 1941).
Records "notable books of poetry and about poetry" published year by year in the U.S.

22.16   Tate, Allen. Sixty American poets 1896-1944. Rev. ed. Washington, 1954.
Lists selected books by and about the poets.

22.17   Braithwaite, William S.B., ed. Anthology of magazine verse for 1913-1929, and yearbook of American poetry. N.Y., [1913]-1929.

22.18   Shapiro, Karl. A bibliography of modern prosody. Baltimore, 1948.
English and American books and articles are listed with brief comments on their contents. Only a few items are earlier than the 20th century.

22.19   Archive of recorded poetry and literature: a checklist. Washington, 1961.
An official list, put out by the Library of Congress, which houses the Archive. Lectures as well as readings of verse are included.

22.20   Gregory, Horace, and Zaturenska, Marya. A history of American poetry, 1900-1940. N.Y., [1946].
Written by poets, not scholars.

22.21   Untermeyer, Louis. American poetry since 1900. N.Y., 1923.

22.22   Rittenhouse, Jessie B. The younger American poets. Boston, 1906.

22.23   Southworth, James G. Some modern American poets. Oxford, 1950. More American poets. Oxford, 1954; N.Y., 1954.
Critical comments on Emily Dickinson, Robinson, Frost, Stevens, Williams, Pound, Elinor Wylie, Jeffers, Marianne Moore, Ransom, Aiken, MacLeish, Van Doren, Cummings, Hillyer, Benét, Tate, Hart Crane, Laura Riding, and R. P. Warren are included in the two little volumes.

22.24   Bogan, Louise.   Achievement in American poetry, 1900-1950.   Chicago, 1951.

A sketch padded out with selections from the poets.

22.25   Lowell, Amy.   Tendencies in modern American poetry.   Boston, [1927].

Robinson, Frost, Masters, Sandburg, H. D., and Fletcher.

22.26   Coffman, Stanley K.   Imagism: a chapter for the history of modern poetry.   Norman, Okla., [1951].

22.27   Hughes, Glenn.   Imagism & the imagists.   Stanford, Calif., 1931; N.Y., 1962.

22.28   Wells, Henry W.   New poets from old.   N.Y., 1940.

The relationship of 20th-century poets, chiefly American, with older traditions in English verse.

22.29   Waggoner, Hyatt H.   The heel of Elohim: science and values in modern American poetry.   Norman, Okla., [1950].

Attention is given largely to thematic discussion and to the following poets: Robinson, Frost, Eliot, Jeffers, MacLeish, and Hart Crane.

See also 32.50.

23. DRAMA AND THEATER

23.1 Baker, Blanch M. Theatre and allied arts: a guide to books dealing with the history, criticism, and technic of the drama and theatre and related arts and crafts. N.Y., 1952.

Entries are annotated; treats U.S. and Canada on pp. 163-190 and includes regional studies as well as works on individual actors and playwrights.

23.2 Firkins, Ina T. E. Index to plays 1800-1926. N.Y., 1927. Supplement, 1927-1934. N.Y., 1935.

Lists published plays written chiefly by British and American authors. (*Play Index: 1949-1952*, comp. Dorothy H. West and Dorothy M. Peake, N.Y., 1953, is a kind of sequel.)

23.3 Hill, Frank P. American plays printed 1714-1830: a bibliographical record. Stanford, Calif., [1934].

23.4 Wegelin, Oscar. Early American plays, 1714-1830. 2d rev. ed. N.Y., 1905.

A list of titles of plays and dramatic poems.

23.5 Roden, Robert F. Later American plays, 1831-1900. N.Y., 1900.

Very incomplete catalog.

23.6 Dramatic compositions copyrighted in the U.S., 1870 to 1916. 2 v. Washington, 1918.

About 60,000 plays registered for copyright. (For titles of plays, etc. copyrighted since 1916, see U.S. Copyright Office catalog of copyright entries.)

23.7 America's lost plays. 20 v. Princeton, N.J., 1940-1942.

A series of previously unpublished plays by a variety of authors.

23.8 The best plays of 1894-1899. Ed. John Chapman and Garrison P. Sherwood. N.Y., 1955.

A brief listing to bridge the gap between 23.20, Odell and the following.

23.9 The best plays of 1899-1909 and the year book of the drama in America. Ed. Burns Mantle and Garrison P. Sherwood. N.Y., 1944.

23.10 The best plays of 1909———. N.Y., 1910———.

Has been continued to date in a series, variously edited, of annual supplements. These contain abridged texts of selected plays, lists of others performed or published, and a variety of other information.

23.11   Lovell, John. Digests of great American plays. N.Y., 1961.
More than a hundred plots are digested, from the 18th century to the 1950's.

23.12   Hamer, Clifford E. "American theatre history, a geographical index." Educational theatre journal, v. 1, pp. 164-194 (December, 1949).
Includes books, articles, and unpublished theses in an inaccurate but still useful list.

23.13   Hartnoll, Phyllis, ed. The Oxford companion to the theatre. Rev. ed. London, 1957.
Contains many entries on American theaters, playwrights, producers, etc.

23.14   A bibliography on theatre and drama in American colleges and universities 1937-1947. Speech monographs, v. 16, no. 3 (November, 1949).
Includes books, articles, dissertations, and master's essays.

23.15   The drama. 21 v. Chicago, 1911-1931.

23.16   Theatre magazine. 53 v. N.Y., 1900-1931.

23.17   Theatre arts monthly: a magazine for the world theatre. 1916———.

23.18   Quinn, Arthur H. A history of American drama from the beginning to the Civil War. 2d ed. N.Y., 1943.
This, with the following item, is the standard work in the field.

23.19   Quinn, Arthur H. A history of the American drama from the Civil War to the present day. Rev. ed. N.Y., 1939; 1945.

23.20   Odell, George C. D. Annals of the New York stage. 15 v. N.Y., 1927-1949.
Covers greater New York City plays, operas, etc. from the beginnings through the season of 1894: first performances, original casts, criticisms. (Since many of these plays went on the road, Odell is valuable also for theatrical history outside the N.Y. area.) The New York Public Library has in scrapbooks a dramatic index covering new plays and important revivals produced in the city between August 20, 1896, and January 1, 1923.

23.21   Hornblow, Arthur. A history of the theatre in America from its beginnings to the present time. 2 v. Philadelphia, 1919.
Contains material not in Quinn.

23.22   Hughes, Glenn. A history of the American theatre, 1700-1950. N.Y., [1951].
A satisfactory general account, marred by inaccuracies in detail.

23.23   Coad, Oral S., and Mims, Edwin, Jr. The American stage. New Haven, Conn., 1929.
A volume in the Pageant of America series.

23.24   Morris, Lloyd. Curtain time: the story of the American theatre. N.Y., [1953].

An informal and popular survey beginning with the early 19th century.

23.25   Seilhamer, George O. History of the American theatre. 3 v. Philadelphia, 1888-1891.

Covers the period 1749-1797.

23.26   Hewitt, Barnard. Theatre U.S.A. 1668 to 1957. N.Y., 1959.

Surveys the professional theater primarily through contemporary accounts. Most of the book is source material, chiefly reviews of plays.

23.27   Moody, Richard. America takes the stage: Romanticism in American drama and theatre, 1750-1900. Bloomington, Ind., [1955].

Contains a treatment of native themes and characters and attempts to relate stage material to contemporary painting, architecture, etc.

23.28   Felheim, Marvin. The theater of Augustin Daly: an account of the late nineteenth century American stage. Cambridge, Mass., 1956.

Daly was a key figure in his day.

23.29   Pollock, Thomas C. The Philadelphia theatre in the eighteenth century. Philadelphia, 1933.

23.30   James, Reese D. Old Drury of Philadelphia: a history of the Philadelphia stage, 1800-1835. Philadelphia, 1932.

23.31   Wilson, Arthur H. A history of the Philadelphia theatre: 1835 to 1855. Philadelphia, 1935.

23.32   Gagey, Edmond M. The San Francisco stage, a history. N.Y., 1950.

23.33   Reed, Perley I. The realistic presentation of American characters in native American plays prior to 1870. Columbus, Ohio [1918].

23.34   Wittke, Carl F. Tambo and bones: a history of the American minstrel stage. Durham, N.C., 1930.

23.35   Graham, Philip. Showboats: the history of an American institution. Austin, Texas, 1951.

23.36   Smith, Cecil M. Musical comedy in America. N.Y., [1950]; [1962].

Plots as well as information on actors and songs are given in David Ewen, *Complete Book of the American Musical Theater: A Guide to More than 300 Productions*, N.Y., [1958], a popular account beginning with *The Black Crook* (1866). See also 19.45.

23.37   Gilbert, Douglas. American vaudeville: its life and times. N.Y., [1940].

A sketchy history which can be often fortified by Joe Laurie, Jr., *Vaudeville*, N.Y., [1953].

Drama and Theater, 20th Century

23.38 Gagey, Edmond M. Revolution in American drama. N.Y., 1947.
A kind of descriptive catalog covering the 30 years prior to publication.

23.39 Weingarten, Joseph A. Modern American playwrights, 1918-1948. 2 v. N.Y., 1946-1947.
A list of plays, arranged alphabetically by authors, plus occasional information on publication or availability of scripts.

23.40 Downer, Alan S. Fifty years of American drama 1900-1950. Chicago, 1951.
A brief survey which covers the earlier years in a rather selective way.

23.41 Krutch, Joseph W. The American drama since 1918: an informal history. Rev. ed. N.Y., 1957.

23.42 Nathan, George J. The theatre book of the year 1942-1950. N.Y., 1943-1951.
Comments on various plays by a popular journalist and critic. Somewhat similar commentary for the seasons 1952-1956 may be found in Eric Bentley, *The Dramatic Event*, N.Y., 1954; and *What is Theatre*, Boston, [1956]. Cf. also John Gassner, *Theatre at the Crossroads: Plays and Playwrights on the Mid-century American Stage*, N.Y., [1960].

23.43 Weales, Gerald. American drama since World War II. N.Y., [1962].

23.44 Price, Julia S. The off-Broadway theater. N.Y., 1962.
Covers the 1920's to 1960; loaded with lists.

23.45 Timberlake, Craig. The bishop of Broadway: the life and work of David Belasco. N.Y., [1954].
Belasco was a key figure at the beginning of the century.

23.46 Kinne, Wisner P. George Pierce Baker and the American theatre. Cambridge, Mass., 1954.
Much detailed information on the background of theatrical history 1900-1940.

23.47 Macgowan, Kenneth. Footlights across America. N.Y., [1929].
Discusses the "little theater" movement.

23.48 Flanagan, Hallie. Arena. N.Y., [1940].
History of the Federal Theatre project with a record of its productions.

23.49 Sper, Felix. From native roots: a panorama of our regional drama. Caldwell, Idaho, 1948.
The bibliography is useful.

23.50 Sievers, W. David. Freud on Broadway: a history of psychoanalysis and the American drama. N.Y., 1955.
Gives separate chapters to O'Neill and Philip Barry only.

23.51   Himelstein, Morgan G. Drama was a weapon: the left-wing theatre in New York, 1929-1941. New Brunswick, N.J., [1963].

See also Caspar H. Nannes, *Politics in the American Drama: Broadway Plays 1890-1959*, Washington, 1960, on plays revolving around a political theme.

23.52   Broussard, Louis.   American drama: contemporary allegory from Eugene O'Neill to Tennessee Williams. Norman, Okla., [1962].

Among other matters, proposes to "establish the attitude of American drama toward contemporary man and his problems": O'Neill, Lawson, Barry, Eliot, Wilder, *et al.*

23.53   Blum, Daniel, ed. A pictorial history of the American theatre, 1900-1956. Rev. 4th ed. N.Y., [1956].

Pictures of stars, producers, etc.

See also 1.18, 4.13, 7.5, 19.43-46, 25.11, 32.12, 32.43-46, 32.70.

24. FICTION

24.1   Fidell, Estelle A., and Flory, Esther V.   Fiction catalog: a list of 4,097 works of fiction in the English language with annotations, 1960. 7th ed. N.Y., 1961. Supplement 1961——. N.Y., 1962——.
Chiefly novels; some translations are included.

24.2   Cotton, Gerald B., and Glencross, Alan.   Fiction index.   London, 1960.
Covers novels, short story collections, anthologies, etc., mainly available 1945-1960, arranged under 3,000 subject headings.

24.3   Cook, Dorothy E., and Monro, Isabel S.   Short story index: an index to 60,000 stories in 4,320 collections.   N.Y., 1953.   Supplement, 1950-1954.   N.Y., 1956.   Supplement, 1955-1958.   N.Y., 1960.
Stories in English or translated into English are listed by author, title, and, often, subject.   The collections indexed number 4,320, plus hundreds more in the supplements.

24.4   Wright, Lyle H.   American fiction 1774-1850: a contribution toward a bibliography.   Rev. ed.   San Marino, Calif., 1948.

24.5   Wright, Lyle H.   American fiction 1851-1875: a contribution toward a bibliography.   San Marino, Calif., 1957.

24.6   Coan, Otis W., and Lillard, Richard G.   America in fiction, an annotated list of novels that interpret aspects of life in the U.S.   4th ed. Stanford, Calif., [1956].

24.7   Griswold, William M.   Descriptive list of novels and tales.   10 parts in 2 v.   Cambridge, Mass., 1890-1892.
Part 1 lists fiction dealing with American country life; part 2, with American city life.

24.8   Gerstenberger, Donna, and Hendrick, George.   The American novel 1789-1959: a checklist of twentieth-century criticism.   Denver, [1961]; [1962].
Lists materials in books and articles on about 230 individual novelists from all periods and follows with a check list of general studies of the American novel.

24.9   Rubin, Louis D., Jr., and Moore, John R. The idea of an American novel. N.Y., [1961].

Excerpts from an array of authors on selected ideas associated with the American background for fiction and on a selection of eminent novelists, from Cooper to R. P. Warren.

24.10   Smith, Frank R. "Periodical articles on the American short story: a selected, annotated bibliography." Bulletin of bibliography, v. 23, pp. 9-13, 46-48, 69-72, 95-96 (January-April, 1960—January-April, 1961).

Deals with the short story in general, not with individual authors or stories.

24.11   Walker, Warren S. Twentieth-century short story explication: interpretations, 1900-1960 inclusive, of short fiction since 1800. Hamden, Conn., 1961.

Few items included were published before 1920, and most are representative of the "New Criticism."

24.12   Thurston, Jarvis, *et al.* Short fiction criticism: a checklist of interpretation since 1925 of stories and novelettes (American, British, Continental) 1800-1958. Denver, [1960]; [1963].

24.13   Cowie, Alexander. The rise of the American novel. N.Y., [1949; 1951].

An impartial treatment ending in the 1890's.

24.14   Quinn, Arthur H. American fiction: an historical and critical survey. N.Y., [1936].

Discusses also the short stories by the chief authors.

24.15   Van Doren, Carl. The American novel, 1789-1939. Rev. ed. N.Y., 1940.

For the most part, outmoded by Quinn and Cowie, but still valuable for its illuminating criticism.

24.16   Wagenknecht, Edward. Cavalcade of the American novel. N.Y., [1952].

From the beginnings to 1940; heavily weighted with 20th-century novelists.

24.17   Pattee, Fred L. The development of the American short story. N.Y., 1923.

Though out of date, still the most consequential general survey.

24.18   O'Brien, Edward J. The advance of the American short story. Rev. ed. N.Y., 1931.

Impressionistic treatment, ending about 1922.

24.19   Leisy, Ernest E. The American historical novel. Norman, Okla., [1950]; [1952].

24.20   Dunlap, George A. The city in the American novel, 1789-1900: a study of American novels portraying contemporary conditions in New York, Philadelphia, and Boston. Philadelphia, 1934.

24.21   Brown, Herbert R. The sentimental novel in America 1789-1860. Durham, N.C., 1940; N.Y., 1959.

24.22 Papashvily, Helen. All the happy endings: a study of the domestic novel in America, the women who wrote it, the women who read it, in the nineteenth century. N.Y., [1956].

A popular study which helps to fill the gap following Brown.

24.23 Lively, Robert A. Fiction fights the Civil War. Chapel Hill, N.C., [1957].

Contains a list of about 500 novels on the war. (Cf. also a catalog of "chief novels and short stories," 1861-1899, by Americans and dealing with the war or its effects, by Rebecca W. Smith, *Bulletin of Bibliography*, v. 16 and 17, September-December, 1939—January-April, 1941.)

24.24 Flory, Claude R. Economic criticism in American fiction, 1792 to 1900. Philadelphia, 1936.

24.25 Taylor, Walter F. The economic novel in America. Chapel Hill, N.C., 1942.

Period covered is 1865-1900. (The bibliography is considerably amplified by Lisle A. Rose, "A Bibliographical Survey of Economic and Political Writings, 1865-1900," *American Literature*, v. 15, pp. 381-410, January, 1944.)

24.26 Jones, Arthur E. Darwinism and its relationship to realism and naturalism in American fiction, 1860-1900. [Madison, N.J.], 1950.

24.27 Fiske, Horace S. Provincial types in American fiction. N.Y., [1903; 1907].

24.28 Åhnebrink, Lars. The beginnings of naturalism in American fiction: a study of the works of Hamlin Garland, Stephen Crane, and Frank Norris, with special reference to some European influences, 1891-1903. Upsala, [1950]; N.Y., [1961]

24.29 McMahon, Helen. Criticism of fiction: a study of trends in the Atlantic Monthly, 1857-1898. N.Y., [1952].

24.30 Parrington, Vernon L., Jr. American dreams: a study of American Utopias. Providence, R.I., 1947.

24.31 Hoffman, Daniel G. Form and fable in American fiction. N.Y., 1961.

A thematic treatment of ten works, by Irving, Hawthorne, Melville, and Mark Twain.

24.32 Lyons, John O. The college novel in America. Carbondale, Ill., 1962.

Begins with Hawthorne but is chiefly concerned with 20th-century novels dealing with college or university life.

Fiction, 20th Century

24.33 Best American short stories of 1915——, and the yearbook of the American short story. Ed. Edward J. O'Brien (1915-1941) and Martha Foley (1942——). Boston, 1915——.

Annual compilation containing texts of selected short stories plus other bibliographical material.

24. *Fiction*

24.34 Hoffman, Frederick J.   The modern novel in America, 1900-1950. Chicago, 1951; 1956.
Criticism rather than history.

24.35 West, Ray B., Jr.   The short story in America, 1900-1950.   Chicago, 1952.
A survey tempered by analytical criticism rather than historical perspective and centered on the 1940's.

24.36 Hartwick, Harry.   The foreground of American fiction.   New York, etc., [1934].
The novel 1890-1930 treated from a New Humanist point of view.

24.37 Simon, Jean.   Le roman Américain au XXᵉ siècle.   Paris, [1950].

24.38 Rose, Lisle A.   A survey of American economic fiction, 1902-1909. [Chicago], 1938.

24.39 Geismar, Maxwell.   Rebels and ancestors: the American novel, 1890-1915.   Boston, 1953.
Norris, Crane, London, Ellen Glasgow, Dreiser.

24.40 Geismar, Maxwell.   The last of the provincials: the American novel, 1915-1925.   Boston, 1947; N.Y., [1959].
Mencken, Lewis, Cather, Anderson, Fitzgerald.

24.41 Wright, Austin M.   The American short story in the twenties.   Chicago, [1961].
Especially Anderson, Fitzgerald, Hemingway, Faulkner, and Katherine Porter; more analytical than critical.

24.42 Beach, Joseph W.   American fiction, 1920-1940.   N.Y., 1941; [1960].
Caldwell, Dos Passos, Farrell, Faulkner, Hemingway, Marquand, Steinbeck, and Wolfe.

24.43 Hatcher, Harlan.   Creating the modern American novel.   N.Y., [1935].
Useful for the 1920's.

24.44 Geismar, Maxwell.   Writers in crisis: the American novel between two wars.   Boston, 1942; N.Y., [1961].
Lardner, Hemingway, Dos Passos, Faulkner, Wolfe, Steinbeck.

24.45 Aldridge, John W.   After the lost generation: a critical study of the writers of two wars.   N.Y., [1951]; [1958].
A somewhat personal treatment of changes in taste and fashion during the 1940's, plus discussion of novelists like Mailer, Shaw, Vidal, Capote, *et al.*

24.46 Geismar, Maxwell.   American moderns: from rebellion to conformity.   N.Y., [1958].
The central focus is on the "transitional decade" from World War II to the 1950's.

24.47   Rideout, Walter B.   The radical novel in the U.S., 1900-1954.   Cambridge, Mass., 1956.
"Radical" means socially or politically radical.

24.48   Bernard, Harry.   Le roman régionaliste aux États-Unis, 1913-1940. Montreal, 1949.

24.49   Gelfant, Blanche H.   The American city novel.   Norman, Okla., [1954].
Dreiser, Anderson, Mrs. Wharton, Wolfe, Dos Passos, Farrell, Algren, Betty Smith.

24.50   Warfel, Harry R.   American novelists of today.   N.Y., [1951].
Sketches of 575 writers "who have published one or more serious novels, one of them in the last ten years."

24.51   Dickinson, A. T., Jr.   American historical fiction.   2d ed.   N.Y., 1963.
Chiefly a list of 1,909 novels, published 1917-1961, classified according to the historical events dealt with.

24.52   Frohock, Wilbur M.   The novel of violence in America.   2d ed. Dallas, [1957].
Chiefly Dos Passos, Wolfe, Farrell, Warren, Caldwell, Steinbeck, Faulkner, Hemingway, Agee.   The first edition announces the limits of coverage 1920-1950.

24.53   Malin, Irving.   New American Gothic.   Carbondale, Ill., [1962].
A consideration of "Gothic" elements in Capote, McCullers, Flannery O'Connor, Purdy, and Salinger.

24.54   Hassan, Ihab.   Radical innocence: studies in the contemporary American novel.   Princeton, N.J., [1961].
Styron, Swados, Mailer, Buechner, *et al.* are dealt with slantingly, and McCullers, Capote, Salinger, and Bellow are treated more substantially.

See also 30.28, 32.26, 32.35, 32.47, 32.51, 32.57, 32.68-69, 35.19.

25. CRITICISM

25.1   Brown, Clarence A., ed.   The achievement of American criticism: representative selections from three hundred years of American criticism.   N.Y., [1954].
Contains also historical introductions and full bibliographies.

25.2   Journal of aesthetics and art criticism.   1941——.
Since 1945 contains in June issues a selective bibliography of current books and articles on aesthetics and related fields, including a section on literature. (For earlier material, see William A. Hammond, *A Bibliography of Aesthetics and of the Philosophy of the Fine Arts,* rev. ed., N.Y., 1934.)

25.3   Pritchard, John P.   Criticism in America.   Norman, Okla., [1956].
An historical survey from the early 19th century to the "New Critics" and "Chicago School"; bibliographical notes, pp. 287-316.

25.4   Stovall, Floyd, ed.   The development of American literary criticism. Chapel Hill, N.C., 1955.
Five professors discuss five different aspects of the subject, 1800-1950.

25.5   Foerster, Norman.   American criticism.   Boston and N.Y., 1928; N.Y., 1962.
Poe, Emerson, Lowell, Whitman; one chapter on the 20th century.

25.6   DeMille, George E.   Literary criticism in America: a preliminary survey.   N.Y., [1931].

25.7   Smith, Bernard.   Forces in American criticism.   N.Y., [1939].
Critics and critical movements are viewed from a Marxist angle as economically determined.

25.8   Charvat, William.   The origins of American critical thought, 1810-1835.   Philadelphia, 1936.
Particularly valuable for its treatment of the influence of the Scottish philosophers and critics.

25.9   Stafford, John.   The literary criticism of "Young America": a study in the relationship of politics and literature, 1837-1850.   Berkeley, Calif., 1952.

25.10   Clark, Harry H.   "The influence of science on American literary criticism, 1860-1910, including the vogue of Taine."   Transactions of the

Wisconsin Academy of Sciences, Arts and Letters, v. 44, pp. 109-164 (1955).

25.11 Johnson, Albert E., and Crain, W. H., Jr. Dictionary of American dramatic critics, 1850-1910. Theatre annual, v. 18, pp. 65-89 (1955).

25.12 Lang, Hans-Joachim. Studien zur Entstehung der neueren amerikanischen Literaturkritik. Hamburg, 1961.

A comprehensive analysis of the period from 1880 to about 1940. Occasionally critics are discussed who are seldom treated elsewhere.

See also 32.78.

Criticism, 20th Century

25.13 Zabel, Morton D., ed. Literary opinion in America. 3d ed. 2 v. N.Y., [1962].

Copious selections, historical outline, lists of recent works in criticism, collections, and names of chief magazines publishing critical articles. Best bibliography of 20th-century American criticism.

25.14 Stallman, Robert W. The critic's note book. Minneapolis, [1950].

Three hundred quotations from British and American critics 1920-1950 are organized into 8 chapters "dealing systematically with central concepts and problems of modern criticism." An extensive bibliography consists of check lists of books and articles topically arranged and includes a section on "Scholarship and Literary Criticism."

25.15 Stallman, Robert W., ed. Critiques and essays in criticism 1920-1948. N.Y., [1949].

An anthology of British and American critical essays plus an extensive selected bibliography of "modern criticism" 1920-1948.

25.16 O'Connor, William V. An age of criticism 1900-1950. Chicago, 1952.

Well-planned but uneven in treatment.

25.17 Santayana, George. The genteel tradition at bay. N.Y., 1931.

Contains unfavorable criticism of the New Humanism. This work was in part responsible for the vogue of the expression "genteel tradition."

25.18 McKean, Keith F. The moral measure of literature. Denver, [1961].

Contains chapters on Babbitt, More, and Y. Winters.

25.19 Weimann, Robert. "New Criticism" und die Entwicklung bürgerlicher Literaturwissenschaft. Halle, 1962.

A systematic treatment, both historical and critical, not confined to Americans altogether and touched by socialist realism.

25.20 Elton, William. A guide to the new criticism. Chicago, [1951].

Explains sources as well as points of view and meaning of terms.

25.21   Hyman, Stanley E.   The armed vision: a study in the methods of modern literary criticism.   N.Y., 1948; 1955, abridged.

Conveys a fair amount of information, with a vast deal of waspish bias, on Wilson, Brooks, Winters, Eliot, Blackmur, Burke, and other American and British critics.

25.22   Fraiberg, Louis.   Psychoanalysis & American literary criticism.   Detroit, 1960.

Individual critics discussed at length are Van Wyck Brooks, Krutch, Lewisohn, Wilson, Burke, and Trilling.

H. A. IRONSIDE
MEMORIAL LIBRARY

26. ESSAY, HUMOR, AND OTHER MINOR TYPES

26.1 Conway, Adaline M. The essay in American literature. N. Y., 1914.
Very elementary; bibliography useful.

26.2 Hicks, Philip M. The development of the natural history essay in American literature. Philadelphia, 1924.

26.3 Brodbeck, May, et al. American non-fiction: 1900-1950. Chicago, 1952.
Uneven and partial discussion of writing in philosophy, journalism, and social theory.

26.4 Blair, Walter, ed. Native American humor. [2d ed.] San Francisco, [1960].
The selections cover the 19th century but the introduction and the very useful bibliography venture closer to date.

26.5 Rourke, Constance. American humor: a study of the national character. N.Y., [1931]; [1953].
Popular work which often goes beyond its title. See also 32.9-10.

26.6 Blair, Walter. Horse sense in American humor, from Benjamin Franklin to Ogden Nash. Chicago, [1942]; N.Y., [1962].

26.7 Tandy, Jennette R. Crackerbox philosophers in American humor and satire. N.Y., 1925.

26.8 Yates, Norris W. William T. Porter and the *Spirit of the Times:* a study of the big bear school of humor. Baton Rouge, La., 1957.
For a generation following 1830 Porter and the *Spirit* shaped the course of the mainstream of journalistic humor.

26.9 Falk, Robert P., ed. American literature in parody: a collection of parody, satire, and literary burlesque of American writers past and present. N.Y., [1955].

26.10 Bragin, Charles. Dime novels: bibliography, 1860-1928. Brooklyn, N.Y., 1938.

26.11 Johannsen, Albert. The house of Beadle and Adams and its dime and nickel novels. 2 v. Norman, Okla., [1950]. Supplement. [1962].
Contains a list of the authors and their novels. The Beadle firm was one of the chief publishers of "dime novels."

26.12   Haycraft, Howard. Murder for pleasure: the life and times of the detective story. N.Y., 1941.
A popular historical survey covering England and the U.S. 1841-1940.

26.13   Wölcken, Fritz. Der literarische Mord: eine Untersuchung über die englische und amerikanische Detektivliteratur. Nürnberg, [1953].
The foreign slant adds slightly to the picture.

26.14   Foote, Henry W. Three centuries of American hymnody. Cambridge, Mass., 1940; Hamden, Conn., 1961.
Traces the story of hymns and their writers, from Colonial times. Supplemented by the same author's pamphlet, *Recent American Hymnody*, N.Y., 1952.

26.15   Thompson, Ralph. American literary annuals and gift books, 1825-1865. N.Y., 1936.
Supplemented by 46 new titles in Alan E. James, "Literary Annuals and Gift Books," *Journal of the Rutgers University Library*, v. 1, pp. 14-21 (June, 1938).

26.16   Cox, Edward G. A reference guide to the literature of travel: v. 2, the new world. Seattle, 1938; 1950.

26.17   Meigs, Cornelia, *et al.* A critical history of children's literature. N.Y., [1953].
Surveys English and American writers. (Helpful also are Elva S. Smith, *The History of Children's Literature: a Syllabus with Selected Bibliographies*, Chicago, 1937; and *Peter Parley to Penrod*, ed. Jacob Blanck, 3d printing, Cambridge, Mass., 1961.)

26.18   Auer, J. Jeffery. An introduction to research in speech. N.Y., [1959].
A handbook on the methodology of research in the various areas included in speech and also a bibliographical guide to professional writing in these fields.

26.19   Speech monographs. 1934——.
Includes bibliographies and an annual record of graduate theses in speech.

26.20   Kitzhaber, Albert R. A bibliography on rhetoric in American colleges, 1850-1900. Denver, 1954.

26.21   Brigance, William N., and Hochmuth, Marie K., eds. A history and criticism of American public address. 3 v. N.Y., 1943-1955; 1960.
On American oratory. Contains also a chapter on rhetoric as taught in colleges in the earlier 19th century.

27. STUDIES OF 17TH AND 18TH CENTURIES

27.1 Stillwell, Margaret B. Incunabula and Americana, 1450-1800. N.Y., 1931.

Lists, pp. 341-440, about 550 bibliographies of and monographs on Americana before 1800.

27.2 Tyler, Moses C. A history of American literature during the Colonial time. [New rev. ed.] 2 v. N.Y., 1897; Ithaca, N.Y., 1949; N.Y., 1962, in one v.

Covers 1607-1765. Though originally written in the 1870's, it is still of considerable use, in view of the paucity of general studies dealing with the period surveyed.

27.3 Tyler, Moses C. The literary history of the American Revolution, 1763-1783. 2 v. N.Y., 1897; [1941]; [1957].

Still the standard work on its subject.

27.4 Wright, Louis B. The cultural life of the American colonies 1607-1763. N.Y., [1957]; [1962].

A social history which establishes close connections with the literary output.

27.5 Piercy, Josephine K. Studies in literary types in seventeenth century America (1607-1710). New Haven, Conn., 1939.

An elementary critical analysis of prose writings to determine what forms of literature were established in America before 1710.

27.6 Clark, Harry H. "The influence of science on American ideas, from 1775 to 1809." Transactions of the Wisconsin Academy of Sciences, Arts, and Letters, v. 35, pp. 305-349 (1943).

27.7 Hornberger, Theodore. Scientific thought in the American colleges, 1638-1800. Austin, Texas, [1946].

27.8 Cook, Elizabeth C. Literary influences in Colonial newspapers, 1704-1750. N.Y., 1912.

27.9 Granger, Bruce I. Political satire in the American revolution. Ithaca, N.Y., 1960.

A survey and an analysis, 1763-1783.

27.10 Wright, Thomas G. Literary culture in early New England, 1620-1730. New Haven, Conn., 1920; 1930.

Not altogether replaced by later studies.

27.11   Miller, Perry, and Johnson, Thomas H., eds. The Puritans. 2d ed. 2 v. N.Y., [1963].

An anthology containing important critical material by the editors on the intellectual background of 17th-century writing in New England.

27.12   Miller, Perry. The New England mind: the seventeenth century. N.Y., 1939; Cambridge, Mass., 1954; Boston, 1961.

A standard intellectual history, continued in the following item.

27.13   Miller, Perry. The New England mind: from colony to province. Cambridge, Mass., 1953; Boston, 1961.

27.14   Murdock, Kenneth B. Literature & theology in Colonial New England. Cambridge, Mass., [1949]; N.Y., [1963].

Strikes a happy balance between "erudition and popular interpretation."

27.15   Jantz, Harold S. The first century of New England verse. Worcester, Mass., 1944; N.Y., 1962.

Corrects many previous misconceptions about the nature and amount of verse produced in the period.

27.16   Howard, Leon. The Connecticut wits. Chicago, [1943].

Trumbull, Dwight, Humphreys, and Barlow; a standard study.

27.17   Levy, Babette M. Preaching in the first half century of New England history. Hartford, Conn., 1945.

27.18   Forbes, Harriette. New England diaries 1602-1800: a descriptive catalogue. [Topsfield, Mass.], 1923.

27.19   Raesly, Ellis L. Portrait of New Netherland. N.Y., 1945.

Discusses, among other matters, the literary productions of the Dutch settlers.

27.20   Tolles, Frederick B. Quakers and the Atlantic culture. N.Y., 1960.

The role of the Quakers in the 17th and 18th centuries. One chapter appears on "The Quaker Esthetic," and there is another on "The Culture of Early Pennsylvania."

See also 22.11, 32.7, 32.15, 32.30, 32.37, 32.40, 32.43-44, 32.64.

28. STUDIES OF 20TH-CENTURY LITERATURE

28.1   Jones, Howard M.   Guide to American literature and its backgrounds since 1890. 2d ed. rev. Cambridge, Mass., 1959.

Omitting the drama, this outline, accompanied by lists of books, is both a bibliography and an attempt to impose order upon the literature as well as the backgrounds. Probably the most generally useful single work for the study of the period. A 3d edition is planned.

28.2   Millett, Fred B.   Contemporary American authors: a critical survey and 219 bio-bibliographies. N.Y., 1940.

A bibliographical handbook, out of date but still helpful.

28.3   The American year book, 1910-1950. N.Y. and London, 1911-1951.

Annual surveys of accomplishments and events; the arts and literature are included.

28.4   Thorp, Willard.   American writing in the twentieth century. Cambridge, Mass., 1960.

A useful brief survey prepared for the Library of Congress series on American Studies; selective bibliography, pp. 325-332.

28.5   Spiller, Robert E., ed.   A time of harvest: American literature 1910-1960. N.Y., [1962].

A series of historical or critical essays by various hands, apparently originally conceived for broadcasting in Europe, which treats briefly criticism, poetry, drama, fiction, humor, and folklore. Has a special chapter on the "New Criticism," by David Daiches.

28.6   Straumann, Heinrich.   American literature in the twentieth century. London, [1951]. 2d rev. ed. London, [1962]; N.Y., [1963].

A systematic survey by a Swiss professor.

28.7   Kazin, Alfred.   On native grounds. N.Y., [1942]; [1956], abridged.

Uneven criticism of prose writers only, from Howells to the authors of the 1930's.

28.8   Fishman, Solomon.   The disinherited of art: writer and background. Berkeley, Calif., 1953.

Speculation on the "impact of culture" on 20th-century American literature: alienation of writers in the 1920's, Naturalism, Marxism, and Agrarianism in the 1930's, the rise of the "New Criticism," attitudes toward Europe, etc.

28.9   Cargill, Oscar. Intellectual America: ideas on the march. N.Y., 1941; 1959.

Considering French, German, and British ideological forces as dominant, Cargill offers suggestions for studying the Naturalists, the Decadents, the Primitivists, the Pessimists, the Freudians, etc. in 20th-century U.S.

28.10   Knight, Grant C. The strenuous age in American literature, 1900-1910. Chapel Hill, N.C., [1954].

A literary history of the decade.

28.11   Cowley, Malcolm, ed. After the genteel tradition. N.Y., [1937]; Gloucester, Mass., 1959.

Various critics discuss a variety of authors or topics treating the period 1910-1930.

28.12   Brooks, Van Wyck. Opinions of Oliver Allston. N.Y., 1941.

A vigorous arraignment of much literature produced 1915-1940.

28.13   Allen, Frederick L. Only yesterday: an informal history of the nineteen-twenties. N.Y., 1931; 1946; 1959.

Very useful for its portrayal of fashions and attitudes of the intellectuals.

28.14   Cowley, Malcolm. Exile's return: a narrative of ideas. N.Y., [1934]; 1951; 1959.

Deals with "ideas that dominated the literary world of the 1920's." The original edition has been considerably revised in the reprints.

28.15   Krutch, Joseph W. The modern temper: a study and a confession. N.Y., [1929]; [1956].

Tendencies in thought in the 1920's and the mood induced by the tendencies.

28.16   Hoffman, Frederick J. The twenties: American writing in the post-war decade. New ed. rev. N.Y.,[1962].

A systematic study centered on 8 themes or trends, with accompanying analyses of 8 illustrative literary texts.

28.17   Whipple, T. K. Spokesmen: modern writers and American life. N.Y., 1928; 1963.

Adams, Robinson, Dreiser, Frost, Anderson, Cather, Sandburg, Lindsay, Lewis, O'Neill. A contemporary appraisal which still has considerable value because of its critical insights.

28.18   Boynton, Percy H. Some contemporary Americans. Chicago, [1924].

Appraisal of writers and tendencies of the early 1920's.

28.19   Allen, Frederick L. Since yesterday: the nineteen-thirties in America. N.Y., 1940; 1961.

Not as consequential as Allen's similar work on the twenties.

28.20   Cowley, Malcolm. The literary situation. N.Y., 1954, 1958; [Glouces-
ter, Mass., 1960].

"A social history of literature in our times"—war novels, paperback books,
how authors earn their living, etc. Cf. also William J. Lord, *How Authors
Make a Living: An Analysis of Free Lance Writers' Income,* 1953-1957, N.Y.,
1962, largely statistical.

28.21   Hoffman, Frederick J.   Freudianism and the literary mind.   2d ed.
Baton Rouge, La., 1957; N.Y., [1959].

Indicates the impact of Freud on certain writers from the U.S. and abroad.
Cf. Norman Kiell, *Psychoanalysis, Psychology, and Literature: A Bibliography,*
Madison, Wis., 1963.

28.22   Duffey, Bernard.   The Chicago renaissance in American letters: a
critical history. [East Lansing, Mich.], 1954.

Covers the period 1890-1930.

28.23   Bradbury, John M.   The Fugitives: a critical account.   Chapel Hill,
N.C., [1958].

Attempts "to set the Fugitive group as a whole in its proper historical
place" and to indicate the nature of the literary work of each member—especially Ransom, Tate, and Warren. See also Louise Cowan, *The Fugitive Group:
A Literary History,* Baton Rouge, La., [1959]; and Rob R. Purdy, ed., *Fugitives'
Reunion: Conversations at Vanderbilt,* Nashville, 1959.

28.24   Writers at work: The *Paris Review* interviews.   Ed. Malcolm Cowley.
N.Y., 1958; 1959.

A collection of discriminating interviews with 16 contemporary authors,
chiefly Americans, including Dorothy Parker, Thurber, Wilder, Faulkner, R.
P. Warren, Algren, Styron, and Capote. A 2d series, N.Y., 1963, carrries on,
with an introduction by Van Wyck Brooks.

28.25   Aaron, Daniel.   Writers on the left: episodes in American literary
Communism. N.Y., 1961.

"A social chronicle of the Left Wing writer" from 1912 to the early 1940's.
Part of a series called "Communism in American Life," of which Clinton L.
Rossiter is the general editor.

28.26   Approaches to the study of twentieth-century literature. Proceedings
of the Conference in the Study of Twentieth-Century Literature. First
session. East Lansing, Mich., 1961.

The *Proceedings* are to appear annually.

See also the subsections on the 20th century under Poetry, Drama and Theater,
Fiction, Criticism, and **15.5, 15.19-20, 15.23-24, 16.14, 21.13, 21.18, 21.22,
30.14.**

29. SPECIAL TOPICS OR THEMES IN AMERICAN LITERATURE

29.1 Spencer, Benjamin T. The quest for nationality. [Syracuse, N.Y.], 1957.

A history of the nationalistic element in American literature from Colonial times to 1892, with emphasis on the period 1830-1860, and a special chapter on Whitman. Contains also chapters on the Transcendentalists and on local-color literature.

29.2 Foerster, Norman. Nature in American literature. N.Y., 1923; [1958].

Chiefly concerned with the 19th century.

29.3 Stovall, Floyd. American idealism. Norman, Okla., 1943.

Illustrates the rise and fall of idealism in literature from the Colonial period to the 1940's.

29.4 Feidelson, Charles, Jr. Symbolism and American literature. [Chicago, 1953; 1959], abridged.

Suggests the belief that "the concept of symbolism" is not only a key to the "situation" of Hawthorne, Whitman, Melville, and Poe but also "a link between their literature and our own."

29.5 Hicks, Granville. The great tradition: an interpretation of American literature since the Civil War. Rev. ed. N.Y., 1935.

Undertakes to show the approximations to Marxism in the literature of the period; strongly Marxist in its criticism.

29.6 Wasserstrom, William. Heiress of all the ages: sex and sentiment in the genteel tradition. Minneapolis, [1959].

A cursory essay that "undertakes to study the genteel tradition, its place in American social history, its effect on literature," especially the novel.

29.7 Herron, Ima H. The small town in American literature. Durham, N.C., 1939; N.Y., 1959.

29.8 Smith, Henry N. Virgin land: the American West as symbol and myth. Cambridge, Mass., 1950; N.Y., 1957.

Various conceptions of the West, especially as they emanated in literature.

29.9 Hazard, Lucy L. The frontier in American literature. N.Y., [1927]; [1961].

Exhibits the excess with which the frontier hypothesis was applied.

29.10   Boynton, Percy H.   The rediscovery of the frontier.   Chicago, [1931].
A semi-popular discussion of the frontier or frontiersmen in criticism and in fiction.

29.11   Cady, Edwin H.   The gentleman in America: a literary study in American culture.   [Syracuse, N.Y., 1949.]
The concept of the "gentleman" as reflected in literature.

29.12   Basler, Roy P.   The Lincoln legend: a study in changing conceptions.   Boston and N.Y., 1935.
Abraham Lincoln in poetry, fiction, drama, etc.

29.13   Bryan, William A.   George Washington in American literature, 1775-1865.   N.Y., 1952.
Record very incomplete.

29.14   Hintz, Howard W.   The Quaker influence in American literature.   N.Y., [1940].
Discusses Penn, Paine, Woolman, C. B. Brown, Cooper, Emerson, Whitman, and "further lines of influence."   See also Tolles, 27.20.

29.15   Turner, Lorenzo D.   Anti-slavery sentiment in American literature prior to 1865.   Washington, [1929].

29.16   Hubbell, Jay B.   "Who are the best American writers?"   Anglo-Americana: Festschrift zum 70. Geburtstag von Professor Dr. Leo Hibler-Lebmannsport.   Ed. Karl Brunner.   Vienna, [1955].
Describes various critical polls undertaken to ascertain the ranking authors in American literature.

30. SELECTED STUDIES OF REGIONAL LITERATURE

30.1 Logasa, Hannah. Regional U.S.: a subject list. Boston, 1942.
Lists of selected books on the various regions, including fiction, travel, biography, poetry, essays, short stories, etc. chosen from material usually found in middle-sized libraries. (A number of the journals sponsored by the state historical societies publish regularly lists of works by or on the authors of their states.)

30.2 Jensen, Merrill, ed. Regionalism in America. Madison, Wis., 1951.
A symposium on various aspects of the subject, containing a chapter, with bibliography, on regionalism in literature. See also, e.g., Howard Odum and Harry E. Moore, *American Regionalism*, N.Y., 1938; Brooks, "Nationalism and Regionalism," *Opinions of Oliver Allston*, 28.12, chap. 21; Robert P. Warren, "Some Don'ts for Literary Regionalists," *American Review*, v. 8, pp. 142-150 (December, 1936); and George R. Stewart, "The Regional Approach to Literature," *College English*, v. 9, pp. 370-375 (April, 1948).

30.3 McWilliams, Carey. The new regionalism in American literature. University of Washington chapbooks, no. 46. Seattle, 1930.
A quick roundup of names and groups.

30.4 American guide series. 1937-1949.
Travel guidebooks for each of the states, a number of larger cities, etc., containing materials originally compiled by the WPA. Various publishers have sponsored them, and a number have been more recently revised. Many of these volumes in their introductory matter contain brief sketches of the literary and other artistic contributions of the localities or states.

30.5 McMurtrie, Douglas C. "Locating the printed source materials for U.S. history: with a bibliography of lists of regional imprints." Mississippi Valley historical review, v. 31, pp. 369-406 (December, 1944).
The WPA sponsored an American Imprints Inventory—listings of the imprints of various states, etc. McMurtrie records these listings to 1943. (More recently, many additions have been made to the recording of local printing.)

30.6 New England quarterly. 1928——.
Contains annually a bibliography of books and articles dealing with the section, including works on literature. (Many items on New England literature of the Colonial period appear in section 27 of this Guide).

30.7 Cantrell, Clyde H., and Patrick, Walton R. Southern literary culture: a bibliography of master's and doctor's theses. [Tuscaloosa, Ala.], 1955.

Coverage to 1948.

30.8 Hubbell, Jay B. The South in American literature, 1607-1900. Durham, N.C., 1954.

Covers not only the Southern authors but other writers who treated the region. Replaces all preceding studies in thoroughness, especially for the period to the Civil War. Its extensive bibliography is filled with valuable comment.

30.9 Library of Southern literature. 17 v. New Orleans, Atlanta, Dallas, [1908-1923].

An extensive, amateurish anthology of selections from numerous authors. V. 15 is devoted solely to biographical sketches of the writers; very inaccurate.

30.10 Harwell, Richard B. Confederate belles-lettres, a bibliography and a finding list of the fiction, poetry, drama, songsters, and miscellaneous literature published in the Confederate States of America. Hattiesburg, Miss., 1941.

30.11 Gaines, Francis P. The Southern plantation: a study in the development and the accuracy of a tradition. N.Y., 1924; Gloucester, Mass., 1962.

Old-South plantation life as treated in literature.

30.12 McIlwaine, Shields. The Southern poor-white from Lubberland to Tobacco Road. Norman, Okla., 1939.

The social history of the poor-whites and their treatment in literature of various periods.

30.13 Agnew, Janet M. A Southern bibliography: Louisiana State University bulletin: Fiction 1929-1938; Historical fiction 1929-1938; Poetry 1929-1938; Biography 1929-1941. L.S.U. Library School bibliographical series, nos. 1-4. Baton Rouge, La., 1939-1942.

The poets represented in no. 2 were all Southern-born; the other lists include also works on the section written by Northerners. In all cases the records are incomplete.

30.14 Rubin, Louis D., Jr., and Jacobs, Robert D., eds. South: modern Southern literature in its cultural setting. Garden City, N.Y., [1961].

Essays on various authors and themes, followed by a valuable check list on 36 writers, compiled by James B. Meriwether. (For material on the Fugitives, see 28.23.)

30.15 Rusk, Ralph L. The literature of the Middle Western frontier. 2 v. N.Y., 1925; 1962.

The standard history and bibliography to 1840.

30.16 Dondore, Dorothy. The prairie and the making of middle America. Cedar Rapids, Iowa, 1926; N.Y., 1961.

History of literature of the Middle West.

30.17   Hansen, Harry.   Midwest portraits: a book of memories and friendships.   N.Y., [1923].
Sandburg, Anderson, Herrick, Masters, Sarett, *et al.*

30.18   Flanagan, John T., ed.   America is West: an anthology of Middlewestern life and literature.   Minneapolis, [1945].
Contains biographical notes.

30.19   Dobie, J. Frank.   Guide to life and literature of the Southwest.   Rev. ed.   Dallas, 1952.
A bibliography with critical comment.

30.20   Major, Mabel, *et al.*   Southwest heritage: a literary history with bibliography.   Albuquerque, N. Mex., 1938.
See also Kenneth Kurtz, *Literature of the American Southwest: A Selective Bibliography*, Los Angeles, 1956, an interesting though inaccurate "reading list of a thousand books which express the American Southwest"; and Edwin J. Gaston, Jr., *The Early Novel of the Southwest*, Albuquerque, 1961.

30.21   Powell, Lawrence C.   Heart of the Southwest: a selective bibliography of novels, stories, and tales laid in Arizona and New Mexico . . . .   Los Angeles, 1955.

30.22   West, Ray B., Jr.   Writing in the Rocky Mountains.   Lincoln, Neb., 1947.
Essays on various authors of the section, with a slight bibliography by Nellie Cliff.

30.23   Davidson, Levette J., and Bostwick, Prudence, eds.   The literature of the Rocky Mountain West, 1803-1903.   Caldwell, Idaho, 1939.
Anthology with a bibliography.

30.24   [Coleman, Rufus A., ed.]   Northwest books.   [2d ed.]   Portland, Ore., [1942].   Supplement, 1942-1947.   Lincoln, Neb., 1949.
Co-operative descriptive lists of works by authors of the region and works on it.   One of the lists classifies titles according to the state or area treated.

30.25   Hinkle, Edgar J., ed.   Bibliography of California fiction, poetry, drama. Criticism of California literature, a digest and bibliography; Biographies of California authors and indexes of California literature. 8 v. Oakland, 1938-1942.
Mimeographed material gathered by a WPA project.

30.26   Walker, Franklin D.   A literary history of Southern California.   Berkeley, 1950.

30.27   Walker, Franklin D.   San Francisco's literary frontier.   N.Y., 1939.
Period covered is 1848-1875, with emphasis upon the 1860's.

30.28   Wilson, Edmund.   The boys in the backroom: notes on California novelists.   San Francisco, 1941.
Reprinted in *A Literary Chronicle: 1920-1950*, Garden City, N.Y., 1956. Cain, O'Hara, Saroyan, Steinbeck, *et al.*

See also **2.10, 3.4, 23.49, 29.1, 29.8, 34.1.**

31. LITERATURE ON OR BY RACIAL AND OTHER MINORITIES

31.1 Porter, Dorothy B. North American Negro poets, a bibliographical checklist of their writings, 1760-1944. Hattiesburg, Miss., 1945.

31.2 Loggins, Vernon. The Negro author: his development in America. N.Y., 1931.

31.3 Nelson, John H. The Negro character in American literature. Lawrence, Kansas, 1926.

31.4 Butcher, Margaret J. The Negro in American culture. N.Y., 1956.

See also Jean Wagner, *Les Poètes Nègres des États Unis*, Paris, 1963, which treats the religious and racial sentiment in verse 1890-1940 but goes wider in its excellent bibliography.

31.5 Redding, J. Saunders. To make a poet black. Chapel Hill, N.C., 1939. Critical survey of Negro poets, from the 18th century to the 1930's.

31.6 Whiteman, Maxwell. A century of fiction by American Negroes, 1853-1952: a descriptive bibliography. Philadelphia, 1955; 1963.

31.7 Bone, Robert A. The Negro novel in America. New Haven, Conn., 1958.

Attempts to "measure the contribution of the Negro novelist to American letters"—since 1853. See also Carl M. Hughes, *The Negro Novelist: A Discussion of the Writings of American Negro Novelists 1940-1950*, N.Y., 1953.

31.8 Gloster, Hugh M. Negro voices in American fiction. Chapel Hill, N.C., 1948.

31.9 Isaacs, Edith J. R. The Negro in the American theatre. N.Y., 1947. Six of the 8 chapters deal with the period 1917-1946.

31.10 Coleman, Edward D. The Jew in English drama: an annotated bibliography. N.Y., 1943.

Includes American plays; to 1938.

31.11 Mersand, Joseph. Traditions in American literature: a study of Jewish characters and authors. N.Y., 1939.

Incomplete account of Jewish authors in 20th-century U.S. (Many earlier works in Yiddish, German, and French are listed in the bibliography of v. 4 of *The Cambridge History of American Literature*.)

31.12 Keiser, Albert. The Indian in American literature. N.Y., 1933.

31.13   Pearce, Roy H.   The savages of America, a study of the Indian and the idea of civilization.   Baltimore, 1953.

31.14   Day, A. Grove.   The sky clears: poetry of the American Indians. N.Y., 1951.

Contains bibliography on North American Indian poetry.

31.15   Robacker, Earl F.   Pennsylvania German literature: changing trends from 1683 to 1942.   Philadelphia, 1943.

31.16   Fenn, William P.   Ah Sin and his brethren in American literature. Peiping, [1933].

Chinese characters.

31.17   Konnyu, Leslie.   A history of American Hungarian literature: presentation of American Hungarian authors of the last 100 years and selections from their writings.   St. Louis, 1962.

31.18   Balakian, Nona.   The Armenian-American writer: a new accent in American fiction.   N.Y., 1959.

31.19   Foreign language press of America: circulation rate and data guide. N.Y., 19——.

An annual listing of foreign-language newspapers and magazines; incomplete.   Includes also the Jewish-American press.

See also 13.23-24.

32. AMERICAN LITERATURE IN RELATIONS WITH OTHER COUNTRIES AND LITERATURES

32.1 Books abroad. 1927——.

A quarterly especially devoted to foreign literature: articles, reviews, lists of periodical articles.

32.2 Denny, Margaret, and Gilman, William H., eds. The American writer and the European tradition. Minneapolis, [1950].

A symposium covering the Colonial period to the present. Two of the 12 essays deal with the impact of American literature in Europe; the others, with the reverse.

32.3 Comparative literature: proceedings of the second congress of the International Comparative Literature Association. Ed. Werner P. Friederich. 2 v. Chapel Hill, N.C., 1959.

V. 2 contains many papers on European-American literary relations.

32.4 Koht, Halvdan. The American spirit in Europe: a survey of transatlantic influences. Philadelphia, 1949.

A "preliminary survey," containing sections on a variety of matters, including literature. See also 8.10, Skard.

32.5 Brussel, Isidore R. Anglo-American first editions. 2 v. N.Y., 1935-1936.

Part I, East to West [1826-1900], describes first editions of English authors whose books were published in the U.S. prior to appearing in England. Part II, West to East [1786-1930], similarly treats books by Americans first published in England.

32.6 Gordon, George S. Anglo-American literary relations. [London], 1942.

A sketchy account.

32.7 Cairns, William B. British criticisms of American writings, 1783-1815. Madison, Wis., 1918.

32.8 Cairns, William B. British criticisms of American writings, 1815-1833. Madison, Wis., 1922.

32.9 Gohdes, Clarence. American literature in nineteenth-century England. N.Y., 1944; Carbondale, Ill., [1963].

Begins where Cairns leaves off and contains chapters on the book trade, periodicals, humor, the vogue of Longfellow, and on critics and influences.

An appendix lists representative articles on American literature which appeared in British periodicals, 1833-1901.

32.10   Enkvist, Nils E.   American humour in England before Mark Twain. Åbo, Finland, 1953.

32.11   Dickason, David H.   The daring young men: the story of the American Pre-Raphaelites. Bloomington, Ind., 1953.

32.12   Boyd, Alice K.   The interchange of plays between London and New York, 1910-1939. N.Y., 1948.

Valuable chiefly for statistics.

32.13   Spiller, Robert E.   The American in England during the first half century of independence. N.Y., [1926].

Includes certain authors like Irving, Cooper, and N. P. Willis.

32.14   Le Clair, Robert C.   Three American travellers in England: James Russell Lowell, Henry Adams, Henry James. Philadelphia, 1945.

32.15   Sibley, Agnes M.   Alexander Pope's prestige in America, 1725-1835. N.Y., 1949.

32.16   Rollins, Hyder E.   Keats' reputation in America to 1848. Cambridge, Mass., [1946].

32.17   Rollins, Hyder E., and Parrish, Stephen M.   Keats and the Bostonians. Cambridge, Mass., 1951.

32.18   Power, Julia.   Shelley in America in the nineteenth century. [Lincoln, Neb., 1940].

32.19   Greer, Louise.   Browning and America. Chapel Hill, N.C., [1952].

(There are many other studies of the reputations and influence of individual British authors in the U.S.)

32.20   Pochmann, Henry A., and Schultz, Arthur R.   Bibliography of German culture in America to 1940. Madison, Wis., 1953; 1954.

Supplemented since 1941 by annual bibliographies listed below.

32.21   Journal of English and Germanic philology. 1897——.

July issues contain special bibliography on Anglo-German and American-German literary relations.

32.22   American-German review. 1934——.

April-May issues contain annual bibliography of Americana Germanica of all sorts, including literature.

32.23   Mummendey, Richard.   Belles Lettres of the U.S. of America in German translations: a bibliography. Charlottesville, Va., 1961.

Originally published in Bonn, this useful book lists only works published in separate volumes—no periodical items or collections. (A list of the latter is promised.) Coverage: from Benjamin Franklin's day to 1957.

32.24 Oppel, Horst. "Amerikanische Literatur." Reallexicon der deutschen Literaturgeschichte. 2d ed. V. 1, pp. 47-60. Berlin, 1955.

Neat summary of the influence of American authors in Germany, accompanied by a bibliography.

32.25 Jantz, Harold S. "Amerika im deutschen Dichten und Denken." Deutsche Philologie im Aufriss. Ed. Wolfgang Stammler. V. 3, pp. 146-205. Berlin, [1957].

A quick survey covering the subject from earliest times to the present, with selected bibliography.

32.26 Springer, Anne M. The American novel in Germany: a study of the critical reception of eight American novelists between the two World Wars. Hamburg, 1960.

The novelists are London, Sinclair, Lewis, Dreiser, Dos Passos, Hemingway, Faulkner, and Wolfe.

32.27 Mönnig, Richard. Amerika und England im deutschen, österreichischen und schweizerischen Schriftum der Jahre 1945-1949: eine Bibliographie. Stuttgart, 1951.

Lists British and American works translated into German.

32.28 Locher, Kaspar T. German histories of American literature: a chronological and critical description . . . 1800-1950. Chicago, 1955.

Printed on microcards.

32.29 Hewett-Thayer, Harvey W. American literature as viewed in Germany, 1818-1861. Chapel Hill, N.C., [1958].

A brief, cursory survey.

32.30 Pochmann, Henry A. German culture in America . . . 1600-1900. Madison, Wis., 1957; 1961.

The most extensive treatment of the influence of German philosophy and literature in the U.S.

32.31 Thomas, J. Wesley. Amerikanische Dichter und die deutsche Literatur. Goslar, [1950].

A brief survey of the entire range of literary influences from Germany on authors from the time of Cotton Mather to O'Neill.

32.32 Long, Orie W. Literary pioneers: early American explorers of European culture. Cambridge, Mass., 1935.

Ticknor, Everett, Bancroft, Longfellow, Motley, *et al.* as students in Germany.

32.33 Vogel, Stanley M. German literary influences on the American transcendentalists. New Haven, Conn., 1955.

(On this topic see also the extensive treatment in Pochmann, whose conclusions are more authoritative.)

32.34 Shelley, Philip A., *et al.* Anglo-German and American-German crosscurrents. 2 v. Chapel Hill, N.C., 1957-1962.

German literature as sources for Simms, Lanier, Howells, and others.

32.35   Marjasch, Sonja.   Der amerikanische Bestseller: sein Wesen und seine Verbreitung unter besonderer Berücksichtigung der Schweiz.   Bern, [1946].

Incidentally revelatory; an appended bibliography lists certain editions of works of Hervey Allen, Louis Bromfield, Margaret Mitchell, Kenneth Roberts, *et al.* published in England, France, Italy, and Germany.

32.36   Mandé, Philippe.   Écrivain U.S.A.; écrivain U.R.S.S.   Paris, [1952].

Contains a list of works in French on various aspects of the U.S. including (pp. 100-102) literature.

32.37   Jaffe, Adrian H.   Bibliography of French literature in American magazines in the 18th century.   [East Lansing, Mich.], 1951.

32.38   Rabinovitz, Albert.   New York University index to early American periodical literature, 1728-1870: no. 5: French fiction.   N.Y., 1943.

A bibliography of articles and reviews concerned with French fiction and published in American periodicals.

32.39   Ansermoz-Dubois, Félix.   L'interpretation française de la littérature américaine d'entre deux guerres (1919-1939): essai de bibliographie.   Lausanne, 1944.

32.40   Jones, Howard M.   America and French culture 1750-1848.   Chapel Hill, N.C., 1927.

32.41   Mantz, Harold E.   French criticism of American literature before 1850.   N.Y., 1917.

32.42   McGee, Sidney L.   La littérature américaine dans la "Revue des Deux Mondes" (1831-1900).   Montpelier, 1927.

32.43   Waldo, Lewis P.   The French drama in America in the eighteenth century and its influence on the American drama of that period, 1701-1800.   Baltimore, 1942.

32.44   Schoenberger, Harold W.   American adaptations of French plays on the New York and Philadelphia stages from 1790 to 1833.   Philadelphia, 1924.

32.45   Ware, Ralph H.   American adaptations of French plays on the New York and Philadelphia stages from 1834 to the Civil War.   Philadelphia, 1930.

32.46   Mason, Hamilton.   French theatre in New York: a list of plays, 1899-1939.   N.Y., 1940.

32.47   Åhnebrink, Lars.   The beginnings of naturalism in American fiction: a study of the works of Hamlin Garland, Stephen Crane, and Frank Norris with special reference to some European influences, 1891-1903.   Upsala and Cambridge, Mass., [1950].

32.48   Salvan, Albert J.   Zola aux États-Unis.   Providence, R.I., 1943.

32.49 Arnavon, Cyrille. Les lettres américaines devant la critique française (1887-1915). Paris, 1951.

32.50 Taupin, René. L'influence du symbolisme français sur la poésie américaine de 1910 à 1930. Paris, 1929.

32.51 Smith, Thelma M., and Miner, Ward. Transatlantic migration: the contemporary American novel in France. [Durham, N.C.], 1955.

More statistical than critical.

32.52 Williams, Stanley T. The Spanish background of American literature. 2 v. New Haven, Conn., 1955.

Influence of Spain and Spanish literature on the nineteenth century particularly.

32.53 Ferguson, J. Delancey. American literature in Spain. N.Y., 1916.

32.54 Manchester, Paul T. A bibliography and critique of the Spanish translations from the poetry of the U.S. George Peabody College for Teachers contributions to education. No. 41. Nashville, 1927.

Record incomplete; appraisal often dubious. Includes Latin American translations.

32.55 Contemporary English and American writers: bibliographical index. By the committee on affairs of cultural and enlightening institutions under the council of people's commissars to the RSFSR. Moscow, 1945.

A list—in Russian—of works translated into Russian, with lists of Soviet reviews of same. It follows *Best Representatives of English and American Literature* (1942), covering the period from the 14th century to the first part of the 20th.

32.56 Brown, Glenora W., and Brown, Deming B. A guide to Soviet Russian translations of American literature. N.Y., 1954.

Based on incomplete sources.

32.57 Brown, Deming B. Soviet attitudes toward American writing. Princeton, N.J., 1962.

A comprehensive and thorough survey, in which Dos Passos, Sinclair, London, O. Henry, Lewis, Dreiser, Fast, and Hemingway are afforded more extended discussion.

32.58 Gettmann, Royal A. Turgenev in England and America. Urbana, Ill., 1941.

32.59 Sinko, Grzegorz. "American studies in Poland." Studi Americani, v. 6, pp. 365-370 (1960).

32.60 Italica. 1924—.

Contains quarterly bibliography of Italian studies in America, including those dealing with literature.

32.61 Shields, N. C. Italian translations in America. N.Y., [1931].

See also Vincent Luciani, "Modern Italian Fiction in America, 1929-1954: An Annotated Bibliography of Translations," *Bulletin of the New York Public Library,* v. 60, pp. 12-34 (1956).

32.62 Peragallo, Olga. Italian-American authors and their contribution to American literature. N.Y., [1949].

32.63 Lombardo, Agostino, ed. "Italian criticism of American literature: an anthology." Sewanee review, v. 68, no. 3 (1960).

Various Italians or Italian-Americans contribute essays on a variety of authors or topics. None of the essays has appeared previously in English.

32.64 Brooks, Van Wyck. The dream of Arcadia: American writers and artists in Italy, 1760-1915. N.Y., 1958.

32.65 Friederich, Werner P. Dante's fame abroad, 1350-1850. Chapel Hill, N.C., 1950.

Contains a section on the U.S.

32.66 Scandinavian studies. 1911——.

The issues for May contain annual bibliography of books, articles, and reviews dealing with Scandinavian languages and literature published in the U.S. or Canada.

32.67 White, George L. Scandinavian themes in American fiction. Philadelphia, 1937.

32.68 Anderson, Carl L. The Swedish acceptance of American literature. Philadelphia, [1957].

Centers on fiction, especially Sinclair Lewis's, from World War I to 1930. An appendix lists Swedish translations of American fiction 1916-1945. See also Stephen E. Whicher, "Swedish Knowledge of American Literature: A Supplementary Bibliography," *Journal of English and Germanic Philology*, v. 58, pp. 666-671 (October, 1959).

32.69 Durham, Philip and Mustanoja, Tauno F. American fiction in Finland: an essay and bibliography. Helsinki, 1960.

32.70 Gergeley, Emro J. Hungarian drama in New York: American adaptations, 1908-1940. Philadelphia, 1947.

32.71 Englekirk, John E. A litteratura Norteamericana no Brasil. [Tulane University, La.], 1950.

Bibliography of both literary and non-literary works translated and published in Brazil.

32.72 Christy, Arthur. The Orient in American transcendentalism. N.Y., 1932.

32.73 Miner, Earl R. The Japanese tradition in British and American literature. Princeton, N.J., 1958.

32.74 Sugiki, Takashi. "A checklist of Japanese journals in English and American literature." Bulletin of the New York Public Library, v. 65, pp. 185-199 (March, 1961).

32.75 The rising generation. 1898——.

A Japanese monthly dealing with English and American literature. In recent years contains an annual bibliography of Japanese books and articles on the two literatures (including translations). The journal is printed in Japanese.

32.76   Sugiki, Takashi. A backward glance at the study of American literature in Japan. Tokyo, 1952.

32.77   North, William R. Chinese themes in American verse. Philadelphia, 1937.

32.78   Pritchard, John P. Return to the fountains: some classical sources of American criticism. Durham, N.C., 1942.

Influence of Aristotle and Horace on 15 writers, chiefly of the 19th century.

32.79   Bush, Douglas. Mythology and the romantic tradition in English poetry. Cambridge, Mass., 1937; N.Y., 1957.

Chapter 15 surveys American poets such as Longfellow, Lowell, H. D., Pound, and Eliot, and a list of American poems connected with classical mythology appears on pp. 577-592.

32.80   Hills, Margaret T. The English Bible in America: a bibliography of editions of the Bible and the New Testament published in America, 1777-1957. N.Y., 1961.

See also 8.10-13.

33. ENGLISH LANGUAGE IN THE U.S.

33.1 American speech: a quarterly of linguistic usage. 1925———.
Publishes articles, reviews, and the chief current bibliography of works in its field.

33.2 Krapp, George P. The English language in America. 2 v. N.Y., 1925; [1960].
Still regarded as a standard study.

33.3 Pyles, Thomas. Words and ways of American English. [N.Y., 1952]; [1963].

33.4 Mencken, Henry L. The American language. 4th ed. N.Y., 1936.
Must be used with two supplements, which appeared 1945 and 1948. A popular account, useful because of its extensive coverage. All three parts were reprinted, N.Y., 1961, as elements of "The American Language Reference Library." An abridgment, made by Raven I. McDavid, Jr., is planned for publication in 1963.

33.5 Craigie, William A., and Hulbert, James R., eds. A dictionary of American English on historical principles. 4 v. Chicago, [1938-1944]; [1960].

33.6 Mathews, Mitford M., ed. A dictionary of Americanisms on historical principles. 2 v. Chicago, [1951]; 1 v., [1956].

33.7 Kenyon, John S., and Knott, Thomas A., eds. A pronouncing dictionary of American English. 2d ed. Springfield, Mass., [1953].

33.8 Publications of the American Dialect Society. Nos. 1———, April, 1944———.
A series of word lists, monographs, etc., such as "The Argot of the Racetrack" (no. 16), "Bilingualism in the Americas: a Bibliography and Research Guide" (no. 26), or "The Phonology of the Uncle Remus Stories" (no. 22).

33.9 Dialect notes. V. 1-6. 1890-1939.
Predecessor of item above.

33.10 Thomas, Charles K. An introduction to the phonetics of American English. 2d ed. N.Y., [1958].

33.11 Kenyon, John S. American pronunciation. 10th ed. Ann Arbor, Mich., 1951; 1958.

33.12   Bronstein, Arthur J. The pronunciation of American English: an introduction to phonetics. N.Y., [1960].
Includes bibliographies.

33.13   Galinsky, Hans. Die Sprache des Amerikaners: eine Einführung in die Hauptunterschiede zwischen amerikanischem und britischem Englisch der Gegenwart. 2 v. Heidelberg, 1951-1952.

33.14   Horwill, Herbert W. A dictionary of modern American usage. Oxford, 1935.

33.15   Nicholson, Margaret. A dictionary of American-English usage, based on Fowler's Modern English Usage. N.Y., 1957.

33.16   Bryant, Margaret M., ed. Current American usage. N.Y., [1962].
About 240 entries discuss one or more points of usage; arrangement alphabetical.

33.17   Evans, Bergen, and Evans, Cornelia. A dictionary of contemporary American usage. N.Y., [1957].
Popular compilation.

33.18   Fries, Charles C. American English grammar. N.Y., [1940].

33.19   Weingarten, Joseph A. An American dictionary of slang and colloquial speech. N.Y., 1954.
Popular compilation.

33.20   Wentworth, Harold, and Flexner, Stuart B., eds. Dictionary of American slang. N.Y., [1960].

33.21   Berrey, Lester V., and Van Den Bark, Melvin. The American thesaurus of slang: a complete reference book of colloquial speech. 2d ed. N.Y., [1953].
Popular compilation, by no means complete.

33.22   Wentworth, Harold. American dialect dictionary. N.Y., 1944.

33.23   Francis, W. Nelson. The structure of American English. N.Y., [1958].
Contains a chapter on American dialects, by Raven I. McDavid, Jr., which is a handy survey-interpretation of the dialect field.

33.24   Linguistic atlas of New England. Ed. Hans Kurath. 3 v. in 6. Providence, R.I., 1939-1943.
Provides evidence of the actual usage of selected Americans in selected communities on selected items of grammar, pronunciation, and vocabulary. Atlases for other regions are in preparation.

33.25   Kurath, Hans. Handbook of the linguistic geography of New England. Providence, R.I., 1939.

33.26   Kurath, Hans. A word geography of the eastern U.S. [Ann Arbor, Mich.], 1949.

33.27   Atwood, E. Bagby.   A survey of verb forms in the eastern U.S. [Ann Arbor, Mich.], 1953.

33.28   Kurath, Hans, and McDavid, Raven I., Jr.   The pronunciation of English in the Atlantic States.   Ann Arbor, Mich., 1961.

Analyzes regional and social features of pronunciation of 157 "cultural speakers," Maine to Florida.

33.29   Herman, Lewis H., and Herman, Marguerite S.   Manual of American dialects for radio, stage, screen and television.   Chicago and N.Y., [1947]; 1959.

Instruction book for actors.

33.30   Sealock, Richard B., and Seely, Pauline A.   Bibliography of place name literature: U.S., Canada, Alaska and Newfoundland.   Chicago, 1948.

Supplements have appeared in *Names: Journal of the American Name Society* for June, 1955, and March, 1958.

33.31   Stewart, George R.   Names on the land: a historical account of place-naming in the U.S.   Rev. ed.   Boston, 1958.

Emphasis is put on the process whereby places were named.   (A selected list of place names with very brief explanations of their origins appears in Henry Gannett, *American Names,* [Washington, 1947].)

33.32   Shankle, George E.   American nicknames, their origin and significance.   2d ed.   N.Y., 1955.

33.33   Carroll, John B.   The study of language: a survey of linguistics and related disciplines in America.   Cambridge, Mass., 1953.

Relationship of linguistic studies with science, psychology, etc.

33.34   Marckwardt, Albert H.   American English.   N.Y., 1958.

A brief, elementary, but clear-headed synthesis of previous investigations calculated to illustrate the "close interaction of linguistic and cultural factors in the growth of American English."

33.35   Hamp, Eric P.   A glossary of American technical linguistic usage, 1925-1950.   Utrecht, 1957.

34. FOLKLORE IN THE U.S.

34.1 Haywood, Charles. A bibliography of North American folklore and folksong. 2d rev. ed. 2 v. N.Y., [1961].

Indexed by state, region, race, occupation, etc. The bibliographies of local sources are immensely useful to students of the literature of the various states and regions.

34.2 Davidson, Levette J. A guide to American folklore. [Denver, 1951]; [1955].

An elementary manual.

34.3 Dorson, Richard M. American folklore. Chicago, [1959]; [1960].

The chief general survey, from Colonial times to the present.

34.4 Funk and Wagnalls standard dictionary of folklore, mythology and legend. Ed. Maria Leach. 2 v. N.Y., [1949-1950].

See also *Folklore Research around the World: A North American Point of View,* ed. Richard M. Dorson, Bloomington, Ind., [1961], also published as v. 74, no. 294 (October-December, 1961) of *Journal of American Folk-Lore.*

34.5 Southern folklore quarterly. 1937——.

March issues contain annual bibliographies, covering principally North and South America. (Other folklore journals of the U.S. include *Midwest Folklore, New Mexico Folklore Record, New York Folklore Quarterly, Tennessee Folklore Society Bulletin,* and *Western Folklore. Texas Folklore Society Publications* is a series of volumes. See Lawless, 19.49, for more.)

34.6 Journal of American folk-lore. 1888——.

Supplements, appearing in April, contain a bibliography of general folklore, international in scope. An analytical index covering the contents of this journal to 1958 appeared in 1958, by Tristram P. Coffin.

34.7 Botkin, Benjamin A., ed. A treasury of American folklore. N.Y., [1944; 1956].

An anthology. Mr. Botkin has edited several different collections—on both city and regional folklore.

34.8 Folk music: a selection of folk songs, ballads, dances, instrumental pieces, and folk tales of the United States and Latin America: catalog of phonograph records. Washington, 1959.

Compiled under the auspices of the Archive of American Folk Song, Library of Congress, which is the chief repository of American songs and ballads. See also Lawless, 19.49, and Wilgus, 19.48.

34.9   Taylor, Archer, and Whiting, Bartlett J.   A dictionary of American proverbs and proverbial phrases 1820-1880.   Cambridge, Mass., 1958.

35. COMPARATIVE AND GENERAL LITERATURE

35.1 Baldensperger, Fernand, and Friederich, Werner P. Bibliography of comparative literature. Chapel Hill, N.C., 1950; N.Y., 1960.
The most comprehensive bibliography of its subject. American literature as a source of influence is treated on pp. 668-681. Supplements enlarging or bringing this work nearer to date appear annually in *Yearbook of Comparative and General Literature,* Chapel Hill, 1952-1960, and Bloomington, Ind., 1961——.

35.2 Conover, Helen F. Current national bibliographies. Washington, 1955.
Lists works which record the current output of books and periodicals in various individual countries, from Algeria to Yugoslavia.

35.3 Index translationum . . .: international bibliography of translations. Paris, 1932——.
Co-operating nations report translations of books to UNESCO, which periodically issues this list. Record incomplete.

35.4 Revue de littérature comparée. 1921-1940, 1947——.
Each issue through January-March, 1960, contains a bibliography of its subject, including latterly a special section on North American influences.

35.5 Comparative literature. 1949——.
Chief American journal in its field.

35.6 Van Tieghem, Paul. La littérature comparée. 2d ed. Paris, 1939.
A standard work for the French school of comparatists. See also Marius-François Guyard, *La Littérature Comparée,* 2d ed., Paris, 1958, a brief and elementary outline.

35.7 Friederich, Werner P., and Malone, David H. Outline of comparative literature from Dante Alighieri to Eugene O'Neill. Chapel Hill, N.C., 1954; 1962 .
An elementary but neat outline, with emphasis on literary influences.

35.8 Hopper, Vincent F., and Grebanier, Bernard D. N. Bibliography of European literature. Brooklyn, N.Y., [1954].
Selected books in English on various aspects of the literary history of Europe, from the Middle Ages to the present century, including biographies, critical studies, and translations of the major authors.

35.9   Van Tieghem, Paul. Outline of the literary history of Europe since the Renaissance. Translated by Aimee L. McKenzie. N.Y., [1930].

The translation was made from an edition inferior to *Histoire Littéraire de l'Europe et de l'Amérique, de la Renaissance à Nos Jours,* Paris, 1946.

35.10   Cassell's encyclopaedia of world literature. Ed. S. H. Steinberg. 2 v. London and N.Y., 1953; [1954].

35.11   Dizionario letterario Bompiani. 12 v. Milan, 1947-1957.

Very extensive and elaborately illustrated dictionary of world literature. General terms, like *expressionism* and *symbolism,* are defined; important works are outlined; a limited group of literary characters are sketched; and a very considerable number of authors are provided with biographical accounts. Works synopsized are alphabetized according to the Italian translations of their titles. A French adaptation is available in the following: *Dictionnaire des Oeuvres de Tous les Temps et Tous les Pays,* 4 v., Paris, 1952-1954; *Dictionnaire des Personnages Littéraires et Dramatiques de Tous les Temps et de Tous les Pays,* Paris, 1960; and *Dictionnaire des Auteurs,* 2 v., Paris, 1957-1958.

35.12   Frauwallner, Erich, *et al.* Die Weltliteratur. 3 v. Vienna, [1951-1954].

Encyclopaedia covering earliest times to 1951, articles on national literatures, literary forms, eminent authors; alphabetically arranged. The bibliographies sometimes help pick up stray works on American authors published in Europe, especially Austria.

35.13   Eppelsheimer, Hanns W. Handbuch der Weltliteratur. 2 v. Frankfurt am Main, [1947-1950].

V. 1 covers beginnings through the 18th century; v. 2 surveys various national literatures for the 19th century and 20th century separately.

35.14   Magnus, Laurie. A dictionary of European literature, designed as a companion to English studies. 2d revision. London and N.Y., 1927.

35.15   Smith, Horatio, ed. Columbia dictionary of modern European literature. N.Y., 1947.

Continental authors and literature from about 1870 to 1940.

35.16   Saintsbury, George E. B. A history of criticism and literary taste in Europe from the earliest texts to the present day. 4th-5th ed. 3 v. Edinburgh, 1922-1929; 1934.

"Present day" means beginning of the present century.

35.17   Wellek, René. A history of modern criticism: 1750-1950. 4 v. planned. New Haven, Conn., 1955——.

35.18   Highet, Gilbert. The classical tradition: Greek and Roman influences on Western literature. Oxford, 1949.

35.19   Olbrich, Wilhelm. Der Romanführer. Stuttgart, 1950——.

Digests of novels and stories; first volumes cover Germany, in particular, and various other European countries. North America, up to 1900, enters in v. 7.

35.20   Thompson, Stith.   Motif-Index of folk-literature.   Rev. ed.   6 v.
Bloomington, Ind., [1955-1958].

Classifies "narrative elements" in folk tales, ballads, myths, etc.

APPENDIX

PRINCIPAL BIOGRAPHICAL STUDIES IN BOOK FORM OF 100 AMERICAN AUTHORS.

ADAMS, HENRY. Samuels, Ernest. The young Henry Adams. Cambridge, Mass., 1948; Henry Adams, the middle years. Cambridge, Mass., 1958; a third volume due 1963.

ANDERSON, SHERWOOD. Schevill, James. Sherwood Anderson, his life and work. Denver, [1951].

BARLOW, JOEL. Woodress, James L. A Yankee Odyssey: the life of Joel Barlow. Philadelphia, [1958].

BELLAMY, EDWARD. Bowman, Sylvia E. The year 2000: a critical biography of Edward Bellamy. N.Y., [1958].

BENÉT, STEPHEN V. Fenton, Charles A. Stephen Vincent Benét: the life and times of an American man of letters, 1898-1943. New Haven, Conn., 1958.

BIERCE, AMBROSE. Fatout, Paul. Ambrose Bierce, the devil's lexicographer. Norman, Okla., [1951].

BRACKENRIDGE, HUGH H. Newlin, Claude M. The life and writings of Hugh Henry Brackenridge. Princeton, N.J., 1932.

BRADFORD, WILLIAM. Smith, Bradford. Bradford of Plymouth. Philadelphia, [1951].

BROWN, CHARLES B. Warfel, Harry R. Charles Brockden Brown, American Gothic novelist. Gainesville, Fla., 1949.

BRYANT, WILLIAM C. Godwin, Parke. A biography of William Cullen Bryant. 2 v. N.Y., 1883.

BURROUGHS, JOHN. Barrus, Clara. The life and letters of John Burroughs. 2 v. Boston, 1925.

BYRD, WILLIAM. Beatty, Richmond C. William Byrd of Westover. Boston and N.Y., 1932.

CABELL, JAMES B. Davis, Joe L. James Branch Cabell. N.Y., [1962].

CABLE, GEORGE W. Turner, Arlin. George Washington Cable, a biography. Durham, N.C., 1956.

CATHER, WILLA. Brown, Edward K. Willa Cather, a critical biography. N.Y., 1953.

CHANNING, WILLIAM E. Brown, Arthur W. Always young for liberty. Syracuse, [1956].

CLEMENS, SAMUEL L. Ferguson, J. DeLancey. Mark Twain: man and legend. Indianapolis and N.Y., [1943].

COOPER, JAMES F. Grossman, James. James Fenimore Cooper. N.Y., [1949].

CRANE, HART. Weber, Brom. Hart Crane, a biographical and critical study. N.Y., [1948].

CRANE, STEPHEN. Cady, Edwin H. Stephen Crane. N.Y., [1962].

CUMMINGS, EDWARD E. Norman, Charles. The magic-maker, E. E. Cummings. N.Y., 1958.

DANA, RICHARD H., JR. Shapiro, Samuel. Richard Henry Dana, Jr., 1815-1882. East Lansing, Mich., 1961.

DENNIE, JOSEPH. Ellis, Harold M. Joseph Dennie and his circle. Austin, Texas, [1915].

DICKINSON, EMILY. Whicher, George F. This was a poet: a critical biography of Emily Dickinson. N.Y., 1938; Ann Arbor, Mich., 1957.

DOS PASSOS, JOHN. Wrenn, John H. John Dos Passos. N.Y., [1961].

DREISER, THEODORE. Elias, Robert H. Theodore Dreiser, apostle of nature. N.Y., 1949.

DUNLAP, WILLIAM. Coad, Oral S. William Dunlap: a study of his life and works. N.Y., 1917; 1962.

DWIGHT, TIMOTHY. Cunningham, Charles E. Timothy Dwight, 1752-1817, a biography. N.Y., 1942.

EDWARDS, JONATHAN. Winslow, Ola E. Jonathan Edwards, 1703-1758: a biography. N.Y., 1940.

EGGLESTON, EDWARD. Randel, William P. Edward Eggleston, author of The Hoosier School Master. N.Y., 1946.

ELIOT, THOMAS S. Matthiessen, Francis O. The achievement of T. S. Eliot. 3d ed. N.Y., 1958.

EMERSON, RALPH W. Rusk, Ralph L. The life of Ralph Waldo Emerson. N.Y., 1949; 1958.

FAULKNER, WILLIAM. Meriwether, James B. The literary career of William Faulkner. Princeton, N.J., 1961.

FITZGERALD, F. SCOTT. Turnbull, Andrew. Scott Fitzgerald. N.Y., [1962].

FLINT, TIMOTHY. Kirkpatrick, John E. Timothy Flint, pioneer, missionary, author, editor, 1780-1840. Cleveland, 1911.

FRANKLIN, BENJAMIN. Van Doren, Carl. Benjamin Franklin. N.Y., 1938.

FREDERICK, HAROLD. O'Donnell, Thomas F., and Franchere, Hoyt C. Harold Frederick. N.Y., [1961].

FREEMAN, MARY E. WILKINS. Foster, Edward. Mary E. Wilkins Freeman. N.Y., 1956.

FRENEAU, PHILIP. Leary, Lewis G. That rascal Freneau. New Brunswick, N.J., [1941].

FROST, ROBERT. Sergeant, Elizabeth S. Robert Frost, the trial by existence. N.Y., [1960].

OSSOLI, MARGARET FULLER. Stern, Madeleine B. The life of Margaret Fuller. N.Y., 1942.

GARLAND, HAMLIN. Pizer, Donald. Hamlin Garland's early work and career. Berkeley, Calif., 1960.

HALL, JAMES. Flanagan, John T. James Hall, literary pioneer of the Ohio Valley. Minneapolis, [1941].

HALLECK, FITZ-GREENE. Adkins, Nelson F. Fitz-Greene Halleck, an early Knickerbocker Wit and poet. New Haven, Conn., 1930.

HARRIS, JOEL C. Harris, Julia F. The life and letters of Joel Chandler Harris. Boston and N.Y., 1918.

HARTE, FRANCIS BRET. Stewart, George R. Bret Harte, Argonaut and exile. Boston and N.Y., 1931.

HAWTHORNE, NATHANIEL. Hoeltje, Hubert H. Inward sky: the mind and heart of Nathaniel Hawthorne. Durham, N.C., 1962.

HEARN, LAFCADIO. Stevenson, Elizabeth. Lafcadio Hearn. N.Y., 1961.

HEMINGWAY, ERNEST. Baker, Carlos H. Hemingway: the writer as artist. Rev. ed. Princeton, N.J., 1963.

HOLMES, OLIVER W. Tilton, Eleanor M. Amiable autocrat: a biography of Dr. Oliver Wendell Holmes. N.Y., [1947].

HOWELLS, WILLIAM D. Cady, Edwin H. The road to realism: the early years 1837-1885 of William Dean Howells, Syracuse, [1956]; The realist at war: the mature years 1885-1920 of William Dean Howells, Syracuse, [1958].

IRVING, WASHINGTON. Williams, Stanley T. The life of Washington Irving. 2 v. N.Y. and London, 1935.

JAMES, HENRY. Edel, Leon J. Henry James: the untried years, 1843-1870. Philadelphia, [1953]; Henry James: the conquest of London, 1870-1881. Philadelphia, [1962]; Henry James: the middle years, 1882-1895. Philadelphia, [1962]; two more volumes due.

JEFFERS, ROBINSON. Carpenter, Frederic I. Robinson Jeffers. N.Y., [1962].

JEWETT, SARAH O. Frost, John E. Sarah Orne Jewett. Kittery Point, Maine, 1960.

LANIER, SIDNEY. Starke, Aubrey H. Sidney Lanier, a biographical and critical study. Chapel Hill, N.C., 1933.

LARDNER, RING. Elder, Donald. Ring Lardner: a biography. Garden City, N.Y., 1956.

LEWIS, SINCLAIR. Schorer, Mark. Sinclair Lewis, an American life. N.Y., [1961].

LINDSAY, NICHOLAS VACHEL. Ruggles, Eleanor. The west-going heart: a life of Vachel Lindsay. N.Y., [1959].

LONDON, JACK. London, Charmian. The book of Jack London. 2 v. N.Y., 1921.

LONGFELLOW, HENRY W. Wagenknecht, Edward C. Longfellow: a full-length portrait. N.Y., 1955.

LONGSTREET, AUGUSTUS B. Wade, John B. Augustus Baldwin Longstreet: a study in the development of culture in the South. N.Y., 1924.

LOWELL, AMY. Damon, S. Foster. Amy Lowell, a chronicle. Boston and N.Y., 1935.

LOWELL, JAMES R. Beatty, Richmond C. James Russell Lowell. Nashville, 1942.

LOWELL, ROBERT. Staples, Hugh B. Robert Lowell: the first twenty years. N.Y., [1962].

MELVILLE, HERMAN. Howard, Leon. Herman Melville, a biography. Berkeley, Calif., [1951]; and Leyda, Jay. The Melville log: a documentary life of Herman Melville, 1819-1891. N.Y., [1951].

MENCKEN, HENRY L. Kemler, Edgar. The irreverent Mr. Mencken. Boston, 1950.

MILLAY, EDNA ST. V. Sheean, Vincent. The indigo bunting: a memoir of Edna St. Vincent Millay. N.Y., [1951].

MILLER, JOAQUIN. Marberry, M. Marion. Splendid poseur: Joaquin Miller, American poet. N.Y., [1953].

MITCHELL, S. WEIR. Earnest, Ernest. S. Weir Mitchell: novelist and physician. Philadelphia, 1950.

MOODY, WILLIAM V. Henry, David D. William Vaughn Moody: a study. Boston, [1934].

MURFREE, MARY N. Parks, Edd W. Charles Egbert Craddock (Mary Noailles Murfree). Chapel Hill, N.C., [1941].

NORRIS, FRANK. Walker, Franklin. Frank Norris, a biography. Garden City, N.Y., 1932.

O'NEILL, EUGENE G. Gelb, Arthur, and Gelb, Barbara. O'Neill. N.Y., [1962].

PAINE, THOMAS. Aldridge, Alfred O. Man of reason, the life of Thomas Paine. Philadelphia, [1959].

PARKMAN, FRANCIS. Wade, Mason. Francis Parkman, heroic historian. N.Y., 1942.

PAULDING, JAMES K. Herold, Amos L. James Kirke Paulding: versatile American. N.Y., 1926.

POE, EDGAR A. Quinn, Arthur H. Edgar Allan Poe, a critical biography. N.Y., [1941].

PORTER, WILLIAM S. Langford, Gerald. Alias O'Henry: a biography of William Sidney Porter. N.Y., 1957.

POUND, EZRA. Norman, Charles. Ezra Pound. N.Y., 1960.

ROBINSON, EDWIN A. Neff, Emery E. Edwin Arlington Robinson. N.Y., [1948].

SANDBURG, CARL. Detzer, Karl W. Carl Sandburg: a study in personality and background. N.Y., [1941].

SANTAYANA, GEORGE. Howgate, George. George Santayana. Philadelphia, 1938.

SMITH, JOHN. Smith, Bradford. Captain John Smith, his life and legend. Philadelphia, [1953].

STEDMAN, EDMUND C. Stedman, Laura, and Gould, George M. Life and letters of Edmund Clarence Stedman. 2 v. N.Y., 1910.

STEINBECK, JOHN. Lisca, Peter. The wide world of John Steinbeck. New Brunswick, N.J., 1958.

STOCKTON, FRANK R. Griffin, Martin I. G. Frank R. Stockton: a critical biography. Philadelphia, 1939.

STOWE, HARRIET B. Wilson, Forrest. Crusader in crinoline: the life of Harriet Beecher Stowe. Philadelphia, 1941.

TARKINGTON, BOOTH. Woodress, James. Booth Tarkington, gentleman from Indiana. Philadelphia, 1954.

TAYLOR, BAYARD. Beatty, Richmond C. Bayard Taylor, laureate of the Gilded Age. Norman, Okla., 1936.

TAYLOR, EDWARD. Grabo, Norman S. Edward Taylor. N.Y., [1961].

THOREAU, HENRY D. Canby, Henry S. Thoreau. Boston, 1939; and Metzer, Milton, and Harding, Walter. A Thoreau profile. N.Y., 1962.

TRUMBULL, JOHN. Cowie, Alexander. John Trumbull: Connecticut wit. Chapel Hill, N.C., 1936.

WHITMAN, WALT. Allen, Gay W. The solitary singer: a critical biography of Walt Whitman. N.Y., 1955; 1959.

WHITTIER, JOHN G. Pollard, John A. John Greenleaf Whittier, friend of man. Boston, 1949.

WILLIAMS, ROGER. Winslow, Ola E. Master Roger Williams, a biography. N.Y., 1957.

WILLIAMS, WILLIAM C. Koch, Vivienne. William Carlos Williams. Norfolk, Conn., 1950.

WILLIS, NATHANIEL P. Beers, Henry H. Nathaniel Parker Willis. Boston and N.Y., 1885; 1893.

WOLFE, THOMAS. Nowell, Elizabeth. Thomas Wolfe, a biography. Garden City, N.Y., 1960.

WOOLMAN, JOHN. Whitney, Janet. John Woolman, American Quaker. Boston, 1942.

INDEX OF SUBJECTS

Bibliography, general aids to, 1.1-14; technical description of books, 3.1-3

Biography, 11.1-23; as genre, 3.12-13; history of, 11.20; of artists, 19.4, 19.7-8; of authors, 11.16-19, 24.50, 35.8, 35.10-15; of journalists, 13.1-3; of musicians, 19.51-53; of scholars, 11.21; universal, 11.1-3

Bohemianism, 10.16

Book clubs, 14.11

Book collectors, 14.1, 14.16; terms used by, 4.10-11

Book illustration, 19.17

Book prices, current, 14.14

Book reviewers, 5.11

Book trade, bibliography of, 6.1-20; history and practice in U.S., 14.1-21; in England, 32.9

Books, published in U.S., 6.5-20; recent, 6.17-19; reviews of, 7.6, 7.13

Books Abroad, 32.1

Books in print, 1.12, 6.19

Bowker Lectures on Publishing, 14.4

Brazil, American works published in, 32.71

British Association for American Studies, 8.10-11

Browning, Robert, 32.19

Bulletin of Bibliography, 1.18

California, literature in, 23.32, 30.25-28

Cartoons, 19.18-19

Catholicism, 18.5, 18.15

Censorship, 15.24

Chicago, as literary center, 21.20, 25.3, 28.22; magazines of, 12.11

Children's literature, 26.17

Chinese, as characters, 31.16; themes in verse, 32.77

City, in fiction, 24.49

City planning, 19.29

Civil War, in fiction, 24.23

Classical tradition, 35.18; influence on American literature, 32.78-79

Colleges and universities, 10.20-22; drama in, 23.14; novels about, 24.32

College English, 2.15

Colonial architecture, 19.30

Colonial literature, 22.11, 27.1-20, 32.7, 32.15, 32.30, 32.37, 32.40, 32.43-44, 32.64

Communism, *see* Marxism

Comparative literature, 35.1-20

Comparative Literature, 35.5

Comstockery, 15.24

Concert management, 19.54

Confederate literature, 30.10

Connecticut Wits, 27.16

Conservatism, 15.16

Constitutional history, 8.1, 10.6

Copyright, 5.5-6; of plays, 23.6

County histories, 9.18

Cousin, Victor, 17.8

Crackerbox philosophers, 26.7

Critics, dramatic, 25.11

Criticism, 25.1-22; abroad, 4.2, 35.16-17; methods of, 2.1, 2.16-18

Daly, Augustin, 23.28

Dante Alighieri, 32.65

Darwinism, 15.11; and fiction, 24.26; *see* Evolution

Dates, general dictionary of, 1.24; in American history, 9.13-14

Decadents, 28.9

Definitions of literary and related terms, 4.1-13, 35.9-14

Deism, 18.7-8

Detective stories, 26.12-13

Detroit Institute of Arts, 19.3

Dialect Notes, 33.9

Dialects, 33.2, 33.8-9, 33.22-23

Diaries, 11.10, early New England, 27.18

Dictionaries, of American English, 33.5-7; of slang, 33.19-21; of various languages, 1.25

Dime novels, 26.10-11

Directories, of cities, 10.24; of newspapers, 13.9-10

Discography, of folk music, 19.48-49; of poetry, 22.8, 22.19

Doctoral dissertations, in all subjects, 1.22-23; in American literature, 8.12, 20.6, 20.9; in history, 9.7; in speech, etc., 26.19

Drama and theater, 1.18, 23.1-53, 32.12; French plays in U.S., 32.43-46; Hungarian plays, 32.70

Drama, The, 23.15

Dramatic critics, 1850-1910, 25.11

Dutch in New York, 27.19

Spanish and American literary relations, 32.52-54
Speech, 26.18-19, 26.21; English language in U.S., 33.1-29
Speech Monographs, 26.19
Sports and recreation, 8.1
Style manuals, 5.3-4
Style sheet, 5.2
Success theme in literature, 15.19
Sweden, American fiction in, 32.68; *see* Scandinavian-American literary relations
Switzerland, American literature in, 28.6, 32.27
Symbolism, in 19th-century writers, 29.4; in 20th-century verse, 32.50
Symphony orchestras, 19.42

Taine, Hippolyte, 25.10
Teaching of English, 2.15
Technical language, 33.35
Television, 13.1, 13.12, 14.1
Textual criticism, 2.18
Theater, bibliography of, 23.1-10; history of, 23.12, 23.18-19, 23.21-23, 28.38-53; in colleges, 23.14; in New York City, 23.20; in Philadelphia, 23.29-31; in San Francisco, 23.32; off-Broadway, 23.44; regional, 23.49
Theatre Arts Monthly, 23.17
Theatre Magazine, 23.16
Theatrical terms, 4.13
Theology, 18.5; *see* Religion
Trace, 12.17
Transcendentalism, 15.3, 17.1-10, 21.15, 29.1, 32.20, 32.30; 32.33,

32.72; magazines connected with, 12.13
Translations, 2.17, 3.14, 32.1, 32.20, 32.23-27, 32.35, 32.51, 32.54-57, 32.61, 32.65-66, 32.68-69, 35.3, 35.8
Travel books, guide to, 26.16, 30.4
Travellers abroad, 32.13-14, 32.32
Turgenev, Ivan S., 32.58
Turner, Frederick J., 10.15; *see* Historiography
Twayne's United States Authors Series, 21.28
Twentieth century, conference on, 28.26; special studies of, 28.1-26

Unitarianism, 17.2-3
University presses, 14.12, 14.20-21
Usage, linguistic, 33.14-17
Utopias, 24.30

Vaudeville, 23.37

Washington, George, 29.13
Weekly story magazines, 12.14
West, as symbol and myth, 29.8; *see* Regional literature
Woman's rights, 10.23
World literature, 35.1-3, 35.10-13
World Wars, 2.2, 24.46, 28.20, 32.39
WPA (Works Progress Administration), 2.10, 7.8-9, 19.9

Yearbook of Comparative and General Literature, 35.1
Young America, 21.25, 25.9

Zola, Emile, 32.48

NAMES OF AUTHORS, EDITORS, AND COMPILERS

Mayer, Frederick E., 18.17
McCausland, Elizabeth, 19.20
McCrum, Blanche P., 8.1
McDavid, Raven I., Jr., 33.4, 33.23, 33.28
McDermott, John F., 2.11
McGee, Sidney L., 32.42
McIlwaine, Shields, 30.12
McKay, George L., 14.15
McKean, Keith F., 25.18
McKenzie, Aimee L., 35.9
McKerrow, Ronald B., 5.1
McMahon, Helen, 24.29
McMurtrie, Douglas C., 14.3, 30.5
McNamara, Daniel I., 19.52
McWilliams, Carey, 30.3
Mead, Frank S., 18.16
Meigs, Cornelia, 26.17
Mencken, Henry L., 33.4
Mendelowitz, Daniel M., 19.4
Meriwether, James B., 30.14
Mersand, Joseph, 31.11
Miller, Perry, 17.7, 21.25, 27.11-13
Miller, William, 14.11
Millett, Fred B., 28.2
Mims, Edwin, Jr., 23.23
Miner, Earl R., 32.73
Miner, Ward, 32.51
Mönnig, Richard, 32.27
Monro, Isabel S., 19.12, 24.3
Monro, Kate M., 19.12
Montague, William P., 16.12
Moody, Richard, 23.27
Moore, Edward C., 16.8
Moore, Harry E., 30.2
Moore, Harry T., 10.16
Moore, John R., 24.9
Morais, Herbert M., 18.7
Morison, Samuel E., 9.10
Morize, André, 2.13
Morris, Adah V., 3.16, 7.2
Morris, Lloyd, 23.24
Morris, Richard B., 8.3, 9.9, 9.13
Morrison, Hugh, 19.30
Mott, Frank L., 12.3, 13.11, 14.17
Mueller, John H., 19.42
Mugridge, Donald H., 8.1
Mumford, Lewis, 19.6, 19.37
Mummendey, Richard, 32.23
Murchison, Carl A., 16.16
Murdock, Kenneth B., 21.4, 27.14
Murphey, Robert W., 1.6
Murrell, William, 19.18

Mustanoja, Tauno F., 32.69

Nannes, Caspar H., 23.51
Nathan, George J., 23.42
Nelson, John H., 31.3
Nevins, Allan, 19.19
Nicholson, Margaret, 5.5, 33.15
Noel, Mary, 12.14
North, William R., 32.77
Northup, Clark S., 20.15
Norton, Dan S., 4.3
Nye, Russel B., 10.2

Oberndorf, Clarence P., 16.19
O'Brien, Edward J., 24.18, 24.33
O'Connor, William V., 21.26, 25.16
Odell, George C. D., 23.20
Odum, Howard, 30.2
Offenhauser, William H., Jr., 3.9
Olbrich, Wilhelm, 35.19
Olmstead, Clifton E., 18.3
O'Neill, Edward H., 7.9, 11.6, 11.20
Oppel, Horst, 32.24
Osborn, James M., 3.5

Padover, Saul K., 15.17
Papashvily, Helen, 24.22
Parker, Donald, 3.4
Parker, William R., 5.2
Parrington, Vernon L., 15.4
Parrington, Vernon L., Jr., 24.30
Parrish, Stephen M., 32.17
Parry, Albert, 10.16
Patrick, Walton R., 30.7
Pattee, Fred L., 21.12-13, 24.17
Patterson, Eugenia, 12.15
Paul, James C. N., 15.24
Paullin, Charles O., 9.18
Payne, L. M., 1.7
Peake, Dorothy M., 23.2
Pearce, Roy H., 22.4, 31.13
Pearson, Norman H., 5.6
Peragallo, Olga, 32.62
Perry, Ralph B., 16.9
Persons, Stow, 15.8, 15.12-13, 17.10
Peters, Rushton, 4.3
Peterson, Clarence S., 9.19
Peterson, Theodore, 12.6
Piercy, Josephine K., 27.5
Pierson, William H., 19.5
Pochmann, Henry A., 32.20, 32.30
Pollock, Thomas C., 23.29
Porter, Dorothy B., 31.1

Post, Albert, 18.10
Powell, Lawrence C., 30.21
Power, Julia, 32.18
Presbury, George P. 13.10
Price, Julia S., 23.44
Price, Warren C., 13.1
Pritchard, John P., 25.3, 32.78
Proske, Beatrice G., 19.21
Provost, Foster, 21.27
Purdy, Rob R., 28.23
Pyles, Thomas, 33.3

Quinn, Arthur H., 20.3, 21.4, 23.18-19, 24.14
Rabinovitz, Albert, 32.38
Raeburn, Ben, 19.38
Raesly, Ellis L., 27.19
Rasmuson, Gunnar, 11.22
Read, Oliver, 19.50
Redding, J. Saunders, 31.5
Reed, Perley I., 23.33
Reis, Claire, 19.53
Richards, Ivor A., 2.16
Richardson, Edgar P., 19.11
Richardson, Lyon N., 12.7
Riches, Phyllis M., 11.2
Rideout, Walter B., 24.47
Riley, I. Woodbridge, 16.5, 16.10
Rittenhouse, Jessie B., 22.22
Roback, Abraham A., 16.16
Robacker, Earl F., 31.15
Robbins, J. Albert, 20.14
Roden, Robert F., 23.5
Rogers, Joseph W., 5.6
Rollins, Hyder E., 32.16-17
Roorbach, Orville A., 6.11
Roos, Frank J., 19.27
Rose, Lisle A., 24.25, 24.38
Rosewater, Victor, 13.13
Rossiter, Clinton L., 15.16, 28.25
Rourke, Constance, 26.5
Rubin, Louis D., Jr., 24.9, 30.14
Rudolph, Frederick, 10.20
Rusk, Ralph L., 3.8, 30.15

Sabin, Joseph, 6.10
Saintsbury, George E. B., 35.16
Salvan, Albert J., 32.48
Sanders, Chauncey, 2.12
Sands, Donald B., 20.18
Santayana, George, 25.17
Schick, Frank L., 14.8, 14.13
Schlesinger, Arthur M., 9.11, 13.16

Schmidt, George P., 10.22
Schneider, Herbert W., 16.1, 18.14
Schnier, Jacques P., 19.24
Schoenberger, Harold W., 32.44
Schultz, Arthur R., 32.20
Schwartz, Murray L., 15.24
Scully, Vincent J., 19.34
Sealock, Richard B., 33.30
Seely, Pauline A., 33.30
Seignobos, Charles, 2.5
Seilhamer, George O., 23.25
Shankle, George E., 33.32
Shapiro, Karl, 22.18
Shaw, Ralph R., 6.8
Sheehan, Donald, 14.9
Shelley, Philip A., 32.34
Sherwood, Garrison P., 23.8-9
Shields, N. C., 32.61
Shipley, Joseph T., 4.2
Shipton, Clifford K., 6.5
Shoemaker, Richard H., 6.8
Shove, Raymond H., 14.7
Sibley, Agnes M., 32.15
Sievers, W. David, 23.50
Silver, Henry M., 5.1
Simon, Alfred, 19.46
Simon, Jean, 24.37
Sinko, Grzegorz, 32.59
Skard, Sigmund, 8.10
Smith, Bernard, 25.7
Smith, Cecil M., 19.54, 23.36
Smith, Elva S., 26.17
Smith, Frank R., 24.10
Smith, Henry L., 13.12
Smith, Henry N., 8.9, 29.8
Smith, Horatio, 35.15
Smith, H. Shelton, 18.5
Smith, James W., 18.2
Smith, Rebecca W., 24.23
Smith, Thelma M., 32.51
Smyth, Albert H., 12.10
Southworth, James G., 22.23
Spargo, John W., 20.18
Spear, Dorothy N., 10.24
Spencer, Benjamin T., 29.1
Sper, Felix, 23.49
Spiker, Sina, 5.7
Spiller, Robert E., 21.2-3, 21.5, 28.5, 32.13
Springer, Anne M., 32.26
Stafford, John, 25.9
Stallknecht, Newton P., 2.17
Stallman, Robert W., 25.14-15

Stammler, Wolfgang, 32.25
Stark, Lewis M., 6.7
Stearns, Marshall W., 19.50
Stedman, Edmund C., 22.2
Steinberg, S. H., 35.10
Stephenson, Wendell H., 10.3
Stern, Madeleine B., 14.5
Stewart, George R., Jr., 4.12, 30.2, 33.31
Stewart, Randall, 18.18
Stillwell, Margaret B., 27.1
Stokes, Roy, 3.3
Stovall, Floyd, 20.17, 25.4, 29.3
Straumann, Heinrich, 28.6
Strong, Augustus H., 18.19
Sugiki, Takashi, 32.74, 32.76
Sutton, Walter, 14.5

Taft, Lorado, 19.22
Tallmadge, Thomas E., 19.28
Tandy, Jennette R., 26.7
Tassin, Algernon, 12.4
Tate, Allen, 22.16
Taupin, René, 32.50
Taylor, Archer, 34.9
Taylor, George R., 10.15
Taylor, Walter F., 21.6, 24.25
Thomas, Charles K., 33.10
Thomas, Isaiah, 14.2
Thomas, J. Wesley, 32.31
Thompson, Arthur W., 8.3
Thompson, Elizabeth H., 4.5
Thompson, Ralph, 26.15
Thompson, Stith, 35.20
Thorp, Willard, 21.2-3, 28.4
Thrall, William F., 4.4
Thurston, Jarvis, 24.12
Tilton, Eva M., 1.20
Timberlake, Craig, 23.45
Titus, Edna B., 12.2
Tolles, Frederick B., 27.20
Tompkins, Dorothy C., 10.6
Totok, Wilhelm, 1.5
Townsend, Harvey G., 16.3
Trent, William P., 20.4
Turpie, M. C., 8.8
Turner, Lorenzo D., 29.15
Tyler, Moses C., 27.2-3

Ulrich, Carolyn, 12.15
Untermeyer, Louis, 22.21
Upjohn, Everard M., 19.32

Van Den Bark, Melvin, 33.21
Van Doren, Carl, 24.15
Van Patten, Nathan, 20.16
Van Tassel, David, D., 9.26
Van Tieghem, Paul, 35.6, 35.9
Van Wesep, Henry B., 16.6
Vigneron, Robert, 2.14
Vogel, Stanley M., 32.33
Von Eckardt, Wolf, 19.39
Von Ostermann, Georg F., 5.4

Wafford, A. J., 1.7
Wagenknecht, Edward, 24.16
Waggoner, Hyatt H., 22.29
Waldo, Lewis P., 32.43
Walker, Franklin D., 30.26-27
Walker, Robert H., 8.5
Walker, Warren S., 24.11
Wallace, David H., 19.8
Wallace, W. Stewart, 11.16
Ware, Ralph H., 32.45
Warfel, Harry R., 24.50
Warren, Austin, 2.1
Warren, Robert P., 30.2
Warren, Sidney, 18.11
Wasserstrom, William, 29.6
Waters, Willard O., 6.6
Watson, Elmo S., 13.14
Watson, Richard L., 15.1
Weales, Gerald, 23.43
Wegelin, Oscar, 22.11, 23.4
Weimann, Robert, 25.19
Weingarten, Joseph A., 23.39, 33.19
Weiss, Irving, 11.13
Weitenkampf, Frank, 19.17, 19.19
Weitzel, Rolf, 1.5
Welch, Walter L., 19.50
Wellek, René, 2.1, 35.17
Wells, A. J., 1.10
Wells, Harry K., 16.18
Wells, Henry W., 22.6, 22.28
Wells, Ronald V., 17.9
Welter, Rush, 14.21
Wentworth, Harold, 33.20, 33.22
Werkmeister, William H., 16.4
West, Dorothy H., 23.2
West, Ray B., Jr., 24.35, 30.22
Whicher, George F., 21.4
Whicher, Stephen E., 32.68
Whipple, T. K., 28.17
White, George L., 32.67
White, Morton G., 15.22
Whiteman, Maxwell, 31.6

23393